THE HOLOCAUST INDUSTRY

THE HOLOCAUST INDUSTRY

REFLECTIONS ON THE EXPLOITATION
OF JEWISH SUFFERING

◆

NORMAN G. FINKELSTEIN

VERSO

London • New York

First published by Verso 2000
© Norman G. Finkelstein 2000
All rights reserved

The moral rights of the author have been asserted

Verso
UK: 6 Meard Street, London W1V 3HR
USA: 180 Varick Street, New York, NY 10014–4606

Verso is the imprint of New Left Books

ISBN 1–85984–773–0

British Library Cataloguing in Publication Data
A catalogue record for this book is available from the British Library

Library of Congress Cataloging-in-Publication Data
A catalog record for this book is available from the Library of Congress

Typeset by SetSystems Ltd, Saffron Walden, Essex

Printed and bound in Great Britain by
Biddles Ltd, Guildford and King's Lynn

"It seems to me the Holocaust is being sold – it is not being taught."

Rabbi Arnold Jacob Wolf, Hillel Director, Yale University[1]

---

[1] Michael Berenbaum, *After Tragedy and Triumph* (Cambridge: 1990), 45.

CONTENTS

ACKNOWLEDGMENTS

Colin Robinson of Verso conceived the idea of this book. Roane Carey molded my reflections into a coherent narrative. At every stage in the book's production Noam Chomsky and Shifra Stern provided assistance. Jennifer Loewenstein and Eva Schweitzer criticized various drafts. Rudolph Baldeo provided personal support and encouragement. I am indebted to all of them. In these pages I attempt to represent my parents' legacy. Accordingly, the book is dedicated to my two siblings, Richard and Henry, and my nephew, David.

INTRODUCTION

This book is both an anatomy and an indictment of the Holocaust industry. In the pages that follow, I will argue that "The Holocaust" is an ideological representation of the Nazi holocaust.[1] Like most ideologies, it bears a connection, if tenuous, with reality. The Holocaust is not an arbitrary but rather an internally coherent construct. Its central dogmas sustain significant political and class interests. Indeed, The Holocaust has proven to be an indispensable ideological weapon. Through its deployment, one of the world's most formidable military powers, with a horrendous human rights record, has cast itself as a "victim" state, and the most successful ethnic group in the United States has likewise acquired victim status. Considerable dividends accrue from this specious victimhood – in particular, immunity to criticism, however justified. Those enjoying this immunity, I might add, have not escaped the moral corruptions that

---

[1] In this text, *Nazi holocaust* signals the actual historical event, *The Holocaust* its ideological representation.

typically attend it. From this perspective, Elie Wiesel's performance
as official interpreter of The Holocaust is not happenstance. Plainly he
did not come to this position on account of his humanitarian
commitments or literary talents.[2] Rather, Wiesel plays this leading
role because he unerringly articulates the dogmas of, and accordingly
sustains the interests underpinning, The Holocaust.

The initial stimulus for this book was Peter Novick's seminal study,
The Holocaust in American Life, which I reviewed for a British literary
journal.[3] In these pages the critical dialogue I entered in with Novick
is broadened; hence, the extensive number of references to his study.
More a congeries of provocative aperçus than a sustained critique, *The
Holocaust in American Life* belongs to the venerable American tradition
of muckraking. Yet like most muckrakers, Novick focuses only on the
most egregious abuses. Scathing and refreshing as it often is, *The*

---

[2] For Wiesel's shameful record of apologetics on behalf of Israel, see Norman
G. Finkelstein and Ruth Bettina Birn, *A Nation on Trial: The Goldhagen Thesis
and Historical Truth* (New York: 1998), 91n83, 96n90. His record elsewhere is
no better. In a new memoir, *And the Sea Is Never Full* (New York: 1999),
Wiesel offers this incredible explanation for his silence on Palestinian suffering:
"In spite of considerable pressure, I have refused to take a public stand in the
Israeli–Arab conflict" (125). In his finely detailed survey of Holocaust literature, literary critic Irving Howe dispatched Wiesel's vast corpus in one lone
paragraph with the faint praise that "Elie Wiesel's first book, *Night*, [is] written
simply and without rhetorical indulgence." "There has been nothing worth
reading since *Night*," literary critic Alfred Kazin agrees. "Elie is now all actor.
He described himself to me as a 'lecturer in anguish.'" (Irving Howe, "Writing
and the Holocaust," in *New Republic* [27 October 1986]; Alfred Kazin, *A
Lifetime Burning in Every Moment* [New York: 1996], 179)

[3] New York: 1999. Norman Finkelstein, "Uses of the Holocaust," in *London
Review of Books* (6 January 2000).

Holocaust in American Life is not a radical critique. Root assumptions go unchallenged. Neither banal nor heretical, the book is pitched to the controversial extreme of the mainstream spectrum. Predictably, it received many, though mixed, notices in the American media.

Novick's central analytical category is "memory." Currently all the rage in the ivory tower, "memory" is surely the most impoverished concept to come down the academic pike in a long time. With the obligatory nod to Maurice Halbwachs, Novick aims to demonstrate how "current concerns" shape "Holocaust memory." Once upon a time, dissenting intellectuals deployed robust political categories such as "power" and "interests," on the one hand, and "ideology," on the other. Today, all that remains is the bland, depoliticized language of "concerns" and "memory." Yet given the evidence Novick adduces, Holocaust memory *is* an ideological construct of vested interests. Although chosen, Holocaust memory, according to Novick, is "more often than not" arbitrary. The choice, he argues, is made not from "calculation of advantages and disadvantages" but rather "without much thought for . . . consequences."[4] The evidence suggests the opposite conclusion.

My original interest in the Nazi holocaust was personal. Both my father and mother were survivors of the Warsaw Ghetto and the Nazi concentration camps. Apart from my parents, every family member on both sides was exterminated by the Nazis. My earliest memory, so to speak, of the Nazi holocaust is my mother glued in front of the television watching the trial of Adolf Eichmann (1961) when I came home from school. Although they had been liberated from the camps

[4] Novick, *The Holocaust*, 3—6.

only sixteen years before the trial, an unbridgeable abyss always separated, in my mind, the parents I knew from *that*. Photographs of my mother's family hung on the living-room wall. (None from my father's family survived the war.) I could never quite make sense of my connection with them, let alone conceive what happened. They were my mother's sisters, brother and parents, not my aunts, uncle or grandparents. I remember reading as a child John Hersey's *The Wall* and Leon Uris's *Mila 18*, both fictionalized accounts of the Warsaw Ghetto. (I still recall my mother complaining that, engrossed in *The Wall*, she missed her subway stop on the way to work.) Try as I did, I couldn't even for a moment make the imaginative leap that would join my parents, in all their ordinariness, with that past. Frankly, I still can't.

The more important point, however, is this. Apart from this phantom presence, I do not remember the Nazi holocaust ever intruding on my childhood. The main reason was that no one outside my family seemed to care about what had happened. My childhood circle of friends read widely, and passionately debated the events of the day. Yet I honestly do not recall a single friend (or parent of a friend) asking a single question about what my mother and father endured. This was not a respectful silence. It was simply indifference. In this light, one cannot but be skeptical of the outpourings of anguish in later decades, after the Holocaust industry was firmly established.

I sometimes think that American Jewry "discovering" the Nazi holocaust was worse than its having been forgotten. True, my parents brooded in private; the suffering they endured was not publicly validated. But wasn't that better than the current crass exploitation of Jewish martyrdom? Before the Nazi holocaust became The Holocaust,

only a few scholarly studies such as Raul Hilberg's *The Destruction of
the European Jews* and memoirs such as Viktor Frankl's *Man's Search for
Meaning* and Ella Lingens-Reiner's *Prisoners of Fear* were published on
the subject.[5] But this small collection of gems is better than the
shelves upon shelves of shlock that now line libraries and bookstores.

Both my parents, although daily reliving that past until the day
each died, lost interest by the end of their lives in The Holocaust as a
public spectacle. One of my father's lifelong friends was a former
inmate with him in Auschwitz, a seemingly incorruptible left-wing
idealist who on principle refused German compensation after the war.
Eventually he became a director of the Israeli Holocaust museum,
Yad Vashem. Reluctantly and with genuine disappointment, my father
finally admitted that even this man had been corrupted by the
Holocaust industry, tailoring his beliefs for power and profit. As the
rendering of The Holocaust assumed ever more absurd forms, my
mother liked to quote (with intentional irony) Henry Ford: "History
is bunk." The tales of "Holocaust survivors" – all concentration camp
inmates, all heroes of the resistance – were a special source of wry
amusement in my home. Long ago John Stuart Mill recognized that
truths not subject to continual challenge eventually "cease to have the
effect of truth by being exaggerated into falsehood."

My parents often wondered why I would grow so indignant at the
falsification and exploitation of the Nazi genocide. The most obvious
answer is that it has been used to justify criminal policies of the Israeli

---

[5] Raul Hilberg, *The Destruction of the European Jews* (New York: 1961). Viktor
Frankl, *Man's Search for Meaning* (New York: 1959). Ella Lingens-Reiner,
Prisoners of Fear (London: 1948).

state and US support for these policies. There is a personal motive as well. I do care about the memory of my family's persecution. The current campaign of the Holocaust industry to extort money from Europe in the name of "needy Holocaust victims" has shrunk the moral stature of their martyrdom to that of a Monte Carlo casino. Even apart from these concerns, however, I remain convinced that it is important to preserve – to fight for – the integrity of the historical record. In the final pages of this book I will suggest that in studying the Nazi holocaust we can learn much not just about "the Germans" or "the Gentiles" but about all of us. Yet I think that to do so, to truly *learn* from the Nazi holocaust, its physical dimension must be reduced and its moral dimension expanded. Too many public and private resources have been invested in memorializing the Nazi genocide. Most of the output is worthless, a tribute not to Jewish suffering but to Jewish aggrandizement. The time is long past to open our hearts to the rest of humanity's sufferings. This was the main lesson my mother imparted. I never once heard her say: Do not compare. My mother *always* compared. No doubt historical distinctions must be made. But to make out *moral* distinctions between "our" suffering and "theirs" is itself a moral travesty. "You can't compare any two miserable people," Plato humanely observed, "and say that one is happier than the other." In the face of the sufferings of African-Americans, Vietnamese and Palestinians, my mother's credo always was: We are all holocaust victims.

Norman G. Finkelstein
April 2000
New York City

CHAPTER 1

CAPITALIZING THE HOLOCAUST

In a memorable exchange some years back, Gore Vidal accused Norman Podhoretz, then-editor of the American Jewish Committee publication *Commentary*, of being un-American.[1] The evidence was that Podhoretz attached less importance to the Civil War – "the great single tragic event that continues to give resonance to our Republic" – than to Jewish concerns. Yet Podhoretz was perhaps more American than his accuser. For by then it was the "War Against the Jews," not the "War Between the States," that figured as more central to American cultural life. Most college professors can testify that compared to the Civil War many more undergraduates are able to place the Nazi holocaust in the right century and generally cite the number killed. In fact, the Nazi holocaust is just about the only historical reference that resonates in a university classroom today. Polls show that many more Americans can identify The Holocaust than Pearl Harbor or the atomic bombing of Japan.

[1] Gore Vidal, "The Empire Lovers Strike Back," in *Nation* (22 March 1986).

Until fairly recently, however, the Nazi holocaust barely figured in American life. Between the end of World War II and the late 1960s, only a handful of books and films touched on the subject. There was only one university course offering in the United States on the topic.[2] When Hannah Arendt published *Eichmann in Jerusalem* in 1963, she could draw on only two scholarly studies in the English language — Gerald Reitlinger's *The Final Solution* and Raul Hilberg's *The Destruction of the European Jews*.[3] Hilberg's masterpiece itself just managed to see the light of day. His thesis advisor at Columbia University, the German-Jewish social theorist Franz Neumann, strongly discouraged him from writing on the topic ("It's your funeral"), and no university or mainstream publisher would touch the completed manuscript. When it was finally published, *The Destruction of the European Jews* received only a few, mostly critical, notices.[4]

Not only Americans in general but also American Jews, including

---

[2] Rochelle G. Saidel, *Never Too Late to Remember* (New York: 1996), 32.

[3] Hannah Arendt, *Eichmann in Jerusalem: A Report on the Banality of Evil*, revised and enlarged edition (New York: 1965), 282. The situation in Germany wasn't much different. For example, Joachim Fest's justly admired biography of Hitler, published in Germany in 1973, devotes just four of 750 pages to the extermination of the Jews and a mere paragraph to Auschwitz and other death camps. (Joachim C. Fest, *Hitler* [New York: 1975], 679–82)

[4] Raul Hilberg, *The Politics of Memory* (Chicago: 1996), 66, 105–37. As with scholarship, the quality of the few films on the Nazi holocaust was, however, quite impressive. Amazingly, Stanley Kramer's *Judgment at Nuremberg* (1961) explicitly refers to Supreme Court Justice Oliver Wendell Holmes's 1927 decision sanctioning sterilization of the "mentally unfit" as a precursor of Nazi eugenics programs; Winston Churchill's praise for Hitler as late as 1938; the arming of Hitler by profiteering American industrialists; and the opportunist postwar acquittal of German industrialists by the American military tribunal.

Jewish intellectuals, paid the Nazi holocaust little heed. In an author-itative 1957 survey, sociologist Nathan Glazer reported that the Nazi Final Solution (as well as Israel) "had remarkably slight effects on the inner life of American Jewry." In a 1961 *Commentary* symposium on "Jewishness and the Younger Intellectuals," only two of thirty-one contributors stressed its impact. Likewise, a 1961 roundtable con-vened by the journal *Judaism* of twenty-one observant American Jews on "My Jewish Affirmation" almost completely ignored the subject.[5] No monuments or tributes marked the Nazi holocaust in the United States. To the contrary, major Jewish organizations opposed such memorialization. The question is, Why?

The standard explanation is that Jews were traumatized by the Nazi holocaust and therefore repressed the memory of it. In fact, there is no evidence to support this conclusion. No doubt some survivors did not then or, for that matter, in later years want to speak about what had happened. Many others, however, very much wanted to speak and, once the occasion availed itself, wouldn't stop speaking.[6] The problem was that Americans didn't want to listen.

The real reason for public silence on the Nazi extermination was the conformist policies of the American Jewish leadership and the political climate of postwar America. In both domestic and inter-national affairs American Jewish elites[7] hewed closely to official US

---

[5] Nathan Glazer, *American Judaism* (Chicago: 1957), 114. Stephen J. Whitfield, "The Holocaust and the American Jewish Intellectual," in *Judaism* (Fall 1979).

[6] For sensitive commentary on these two contrasting types of survivor, see Primo Levi, *The Reawakening*, with a new afterword (New York: 1986), 207.

[7] In this text, *Jewish elites* designates individuals prominent in the organizational and cultural life of the mainstream Jewish community.

policy. Doing so in effect facilitated the traditional goals of assimilation and access to power. With the inception of the Cold War, mainstream Jewish organizations jumped into the fray. American Jewish elites "forgot" the Nazi holocaust because Germany – West Germany by 1949 – became a crucial postwar American ally in the US confrontation with the Soviet Union. Dredging up the past served no useful purpose; in fact it complicated matters.

With minor reservations (soon discarded), major American Jewish organizations quickly fell into line with US support for a rearmed and barely de-Nazified Germany. The American Jewish Committee (AJC), fearful that "any organized opposition of American Jews against the new foreign policy and strategic approach could isolate them in the eyes of the non-Jewish majority and endanger their postwar achievements on the domestic scene," was the first to preach the virtues of realignment. The pro-Zionist World Jewish Congress (WJC) and its American affiliate dropped opposition after signing compensation agreements with Germany in the early 1950s, while the Anti-Defamation League (ADL) was the first major Jewish organization to send an official delegation to Germany, in 1954. Together these organizations collaborated with the Bonn government to contain the "anti-German wave" of Jewish popular sentiment.[8]

The Final Solution was a taboo topic of American Jewish elites for yet another reason. Leftist Jews, who were opposed to the Cold War alignment with Germany against the Soviet Union, would not stop

---

[8] Shlomo Shafir, *Ambiguous Relations: The American Jewish Community and Germany Since 1945* (Detroit: 1999), 88, 98, 100–1, 111, 113, 114, 177, 192, 215, 231, 251.

harping on it. Remembrance of the Nazi holocaust was tagged as a Communist cause. Strapped with the stereotype that conflated Jews with the Left – in fact, Jews did account for a third of the vote for progressive presidential candidate Henry Wallace in 1948 – American Jewish elites did not shrink from sacrificing fellow Jews on the altar of anti-Communism. Offering their files on alleged Jewish subversives to government agencies, the AJC and the ADL actively collaborated in the McCarthy-era witch-hunt. The AJC endorsed the death penalty for the Rosenbergs, while its monthly publication, *Commentary*, editorialized that they weren't *really* Jews.

Fearful of association with the political Left abroad and at home, mainstream Jewish organizations opposed cooperation with anti-Nazi German social-democrats as well as boycotts of German manufactures and public demonstrations against ex-Nazis touring the United States. On the other hand, prominent visiting German dissidents like Protestant pastor Martin Niemöller, who had spent eight years in Nazi concentration camps and was now against the anti-Communist crusade, suffered the obloquy of American Jewish leaders. Anxious to boost their anti-Communist credentials, Jewish elites even enlisted in, and financially sustained, right-wing extremist organizations like the All-American Conference to Combat Communism and turned a blind eye as veterans of the Nazi SS entered the country.[9]

[9] Ibid., 98, 106, 123–37, 205, 215–16, 249. Robert Warshaw, "The 'Idealism' of Julius and Ethel Rosenberg," in *Commentary* (November 1953). Was it merely a coincidence that at the same time, mainstream Jewish organizations crucified Hannah Arendt for pointing up the collaboration of aggrandizing Jewish elites during the Nazi era? Recalling the perfidious role of the Jewish Council police force, Yitzhak Zuckerman, a leader of the Warsaw Ghetto

Ever anxious to ingratiate themselves with US ruling elites and dissociate themselves from the Jewish Left, organized American Jewry did invoke the Nazi holocaust in one special context: to denounce the USSR. "Soviet [anti-Jewish] policy opens up opportunities which must not be overlooked," an internal AJC memorandum quoted by Novick gleefully noted, "to reinforce certain aspects of AJC domestic program." Typically, that meant bracketing the Nazi Final Solution with Russian anti-Semitism. "Stalin will succeed where Hitler failed," *Commentary* direly predicted. "He will finally wipe out the Jews of Central and Eastern Europe. . . . The parallel with the policy of Nazi extermination is almost complete." Major American Jewish organizations even denounced the 1956 Soviet invasion of Hungary as "only the first station on the way to a Russian Auschwitz."[10]

~

Everything changed with the June 1967 Arab–Israeli war. By virtually all accounts, it was only after this conflict that The Holocaust became a fixture in American Jewish life.[11] The standard explanation of this

---

uprising, observed: 'There weren't any 'decent' policemen because decent men took off the uniform and became simple Jews" (*A Surplus of Memory* [Oxford: 1993], 244).

[10] Novick, *The Holocaust*, 98–100. In addition to the Cold War, other factors played an ancillary role in American Jewry's postwar downplaying of the Nazi holocaust – for example, fear of anti-Semitism, and the optimistic, assimilationist American ethos in the 1950s. Novick explores these matters in chapters 4–7 of *The Holocaust*.

[11] Apparently the only one denying this connection is Elie Wiesel, who claims that the emergence of The Holocaust in American life was primarily his doing. (Saidel, *Never Too Late*, 33–4)

transformation is that Israel's extreme isolation and vulnerability during the June war revived memories of the Nazi extermination. In fact, this analysis misrepresents both the reality of Mideast power relations at the time and the nature of the evolving relationship between American Jewish elites and Israel.

Just as mainstream American Jewish organizations downplayed the Nazi holocaust in the years after World War II to conform to the US government's Cold War priorities, so their attitude to Israel kept in step with US policy. From early on, American Jewish elites harbored profound misgivings about a Jewish state. Uppermost was their fear that it would lend credence to the "dual loyalty" charge. As the Cold War intensified, these worries multiplied. Already before the founding of Israel, American Jewish leaders voiced concern that its largely Eastern European, left-wing leadership would join the Soviet camp. Although they eventually embraced the Zionist-led campaign for statehood, American Jewish organizations closely monitored and adjusted to signals from Washington. Indeed, the AJC supported Israel's founding mainly out of fear that a domestic backlash against Jews might ensue if the Jewish DPs in Europe were not quickly settled.[12] Although Israel aligned with the West soon after the state was formed, many Israelis in and out of government retained strong affection for the Soviet Union; predictably, American Jewish leaders kept Israel at arm's length.

From its founding in 1948 through the June 1967 war, Israel did not figure centrally in American strategic planning. As the Palestinian Jewish leadership prepared to declare statehood, President Truman

---

[12] Menahem Kaufman, *An Ambiguous Partnership* (Jerusalem: 1991), 218, 276–7.

waffled, weighing domestic considerations (the Jewish vote) against State Department alarm (support for a Jewish state would alienate the Arab world). To secure US interests in the Middle East, the Eisenhower Administration balanced support for Israel and for Arab nations, favoring, however, the Arabs.

Intermittent Israeli clashes with the United States over policy issues culminated in the Suez crisis of 1956, when Israel colluded with Britain and France to attack Egypt's nationalist leader, Gamal Abdel Nasser. Although Israel's lightning victory and seizure of the Sinai Peninsula drew general attention to its strategic potential, the United States still counted it as only one among several regional assets. Accordingly, President Eisenhower forced Israel's full, virtually unconditional withdrawal from the Sinai. During the crisis, American Jewish leaders did briefly back Israeli efforts to wrest American concessions, but ultimately, as Arthur Hertzberg recalls, they "preferred to counsel Israel to heed [Eisenhower] rather than oppose the wishes of the leader of the United States."[13]

Except as an occasional object of charity, Israel practically dropped from sight in American Jewish life soon after the founding of the state. In fact, Israel was not important to American Jews. In his 1957 survey, Nathan Glazer reported that Israel "had remarkably slight effects on the inner life of American Jewry."[14] Membership in the Zionist Organ-

---

[13] Arthur Hertzberg, *Jewish Polemics* (New York: 1992), 33; although misleadingly apologetic, cf. Isaac Alteras, "Eisenhower, American Jewry, and Israel," in *American Jewish Archives* (November 1985), and Michael Reiner, "The Reaction of US Jewish Organizations to the Sinai Campaign and Its Aftermath," in *Forum* (Winter 1980–1).

[14] Nathan Glazer, *American Judaism* (Chicago: 1957), 114. Glazer continued:

ization of America dropped from the hundreds of thousands in 1948 to the tens of thousands in the 1960s. Only 1 in 20 American Jews cared to visit Israel before June 1967. In his 1956 reelection, which occurred immediately after he forced Israel's humiliating withdrawal from the Sinai, the already considerable Jewish support for Eisenhower increased. In the early 1960s, Israel even faced a drubbing for the Eichmann kidnaping from sections of elite Jewish opinion like Joseph Proskauer, past president of the AJC, Harvard historian Oscar Handlin and the Jewish-owned *Washington Post*. "The kidnaping of Eichmann," Erich Fromm opined, "is an act of lawlessness of exactly the type of which the Nazis themselves . . . have been guilty."[15]

Across the political spectrum, American Jewish intellectuals proved especially indifferent to Israel's fate. Detailed studies of the left-liberal New York Jewish intellectual scene through the 1960s barely mention Israel.[16] Just before the June war, the AJC sponsored a symposium on "Jewish Identity Here and Now." Only three of the thirty-one "best minds in the Jewish community" even alluded to Israel; two of them did so only to dismiss its relevance.[17] Telling irony: just about the only two public Jewish intellectuals who had forged a bond with Israel before June 1967 were Hannah Arendt and Noam Chomsky.[18]

"Israel has meant almost nothing for American Judaism. . . . [T]he idea that Israel . . . could in any serious way affect Judaism in America . . . is recognized as illusory" (115).

[15] Shafir, *Ambiguous Relations*, 222.

[16] See, for example, Alexander Bloom, *Prodigal Sons* (New York: 1986).

[17] Lucy Dawidowicz and Milton Himmelfarb (eds), *Conference on Jewish Identity Here and Now* (American Jewish Committee: 1967).

[18] After emigrating from Germany in 1933, Arendt became an activist in the

Then came the June war. Impressed by Israel's overwhelming display of force, the United States moved to incorporate it as a strategic asset. (Already before the June war the United States had cautiously tilted toward Israel as the Egyptian and Syrian regimes charted an increasingly independent course in the mid-1960s.) Military and economic assistance began to pour in as Israel turned into a proxy for US power in the Middle East.

For American Jewish elites, Israel's subordination to US power was a windfall. Zionism had sprung from the premise that assimilation was a pipe dream, that Jews would always be perceived as potentially disloyal aliens. To resolve this dilemma, Zionists sought to establish a homeland for the Jews. In fact, Israel's founding exacerbated the problem, at any rate for diaspora Jewry: it gave the charge of dual loyalty institutional expression. Paradoxically, after June 1967, Israel *facilitated* assimilation in the United States: Jews now stood on the front lines defending America – indeed, "Western civilization" – against the retrograde Arab hordes. Whereas before 1967 Israel conjured the bogy of dual loyalty, it now connoted super-loyalty. After all, it was not Americans but Israelis fighting and

French Zionist movement; during World War II through Israel's founding, she wrote extensively on Zionism. The son of a prominent American Hebraist, Chomsky was raised in a Zionist home and, shortly after Israel's independence, spent time on a kibbutz. Both the public campaigns vilifying Arendt in the early 1960s and Chomsky in the 1970s were spearheaded by the ADL. (Elisabeth Young-Bruehl, *Hannah Arendt* [New Haven: 1982], 105–8, 138–9, 143–4, 182–4, 223–33, 348; Robert F. Barsky, *Noam Chomsky* [Cambridge: 1997], 9–93; David Barsamian (ed.), *Chronicles of Dissent* [Monroe, ME: 1992], 38) dying to protect US interests. And unlike the American GIs in Vietnam, Israeli fighters were not being humiliated by Third World upstarts.[19]

Accordingly, American Jewish elites suddenly discovered Israel. After the 1967 war, Israel's military élan could be celebrated because its guns pointed in the right direction – against America's enemies. Its martial prowess might even facilitate entry into the inner sanctums of American power. Previously Jewish elites could only offer a few lists of Jewish subversives; now, they could pose as the natural interlocutors for America's newest strategic asset. From bit players, they could advance to top billing in the Cold War drama. Thus for American Jewry, as well as the United States, Israel became a strategic asset.

In a memoir published just before the June war, Norman Podhoretz giddily recalled attending a state dinner at the White House that "included not a single person who was not visibly and absolutely beside himself with delight to be there."[20] Although already editor of the leading American Jewish periodical, *Commentary*, his memoir includes only one fleeting allusion to Israel. What did Israel have to offer an ambitious American Jew? In a later memoir, Podhoretz remembered that after June 1967 Israel became "the religion of the American Jews."[21] Now a prominent supporter of Israel, Podhoretz could boast not merely of attending a White House dinner but of

[19] For an early prefiguration of my argument, see Hannah Arendt, "Zionism Reconsidered" (1944), in Ron Feldman (ed.), *The Jew as Pariah* (New York: 1978), 159.

[20] *Making It* (New York: 1967), 336.

[21] *Breaking Ranks* (New York: 1979), 335.

meeting tête-à-tête with the President to deliberate on the National Interest.

After the June war, mainstream American Jewish organizations worked full time to firm up the American–Israeli alliance. In the case of the ADL, this included a far-flung domestic surveillance operation with ties to Israeli and South African intelligence.[22] Coverage of Israel in *The New York Times* increased dramatically after June 1967. The 1955 and 1965 entries for Israel in *The New York Times Index* each filled 60 column inches. The entry for Israel in 1975 ran to fully 260 column inches. "When I want to feel better," Wiesel reflected in 1973, "I turn to the Israeli items in *The New York Times*."[23] Like Podhoretz, many mainstream American Jewish intellectuals also suddenly found "religion" after the June war. Novick reports that Lucy Dawidowicz, the doyenne of Holocaust literature, had once been a "sharp critic of Israel." Israel could not demand reparations from Germany, she railed in 1953, while evading responsibility for displaced Palestinians: "Morality cannot be that flexible." Yet almost immediately after the June war, Dawidowicz became a "fervent supporter of Israel," acclaiming it as "the corporate paradigm for the ideal image of the Jew in the modern world."[24]

[22] Robert I. Friedman, "The Anti-Defamation League Is Spying on You," in *Village Voice* (11 May 1993). Abdeen Jabara, "The Anti-Defamation League: Civil Rights and Wrongs," in *CovertAction* (Summer 1993). Matt Isaacs, "Spy vs Spite," in *SF Weekly* (2–8 February 2000).

[23] Elie Wiesel, *Against Silence*, selected and edited by Irving Abrahamson (New York: 1984), v. i, 283.

[24] Novick, *The Holocaust*, 147. Lucy S. Dawidowicz, *The Jewish Presence* (New York: 1977), 26.

A favorite posture of the post-1967 born-again Zionists was tacitly to juxtapose their own outspoken support for a supposedly beleaguered Israel against the cravenness of American Jewry during The Holocaust. In fact, they were doing exactly what American Jewish elites had always done: marching in lockstep with American power. The educated classes proved particularly adept at striking heroic poses. Consider the prominent left-liberal social critic Irving Howe. In 1956 the journal Howe edited, *Dissent*, condemned the "combined attack on Egypt" as "immoral." Although truly standing alone, Israel was also taken to task for "cultural chauvinism," a "quasi-messianic sense of manifest destiny," and "an undercurrent of expansionism."[25] After the October 1973 war, when American support for Israel peaked, Howe published a personal manifesto "filled with anxiety so intense" in defense of isolated Israel. The Gentile world, he lamented in a Woody Allen-like parody, was awash with anti-Semitism. Even in Upper Manhattan, he lamented, Israel was "no longer chic": everyone, apart from himself, was allegedly in thrall to Mao, Fanon and Guevara.[26]

As America's strategic asset, Israel was not without critics. Besides the increasing international censure of its refusal to negotiate a settlement with the Arabs in accordance with United Nations resolutions and its truculent support of American global ambitions,[27] Israel had to cope with domestic US dissent as well. In American ruling circles,

---

[25] "Eruption in the Middle East," in *Dissent* (Winter 1957).

[26] "Israel: Thinking the Unthinkable," in *New York* magazine (24 December 1973).

[27] Norman G. Finkelstein, *Image and Reality of the Israel–Palestine Conflict* (New York: 1995), chaps 5–6.

so-called Arabists maintained that putting all the eggs in the Israel basket while ignoring Arab elites undermined US national interests.

Some argued that Israel's subordination to US power and occupation of neighboring Arab states were not only wrong in principle but also harmful to its own interests. Israel would become increasingly militarized and alienated from the Arab world. For Israel's new American Jewish "supporters," however, such talk bordered on heresy: an independent Israel at peace with its neighbors was worthless; an Israel aligned with currents in the Arab world seeking independence from the United States was a disaster. Only an Israeli Sparta beholden to American power would do, because only then could US Jewish leaders act as the spokesmen for American imperial ambitions. Noam Chomsky has suggested that these "supporters of Israel" should more properly be called "supporters of the moral degeneration and ultimate destruction of Israel."[28]

To protect their strategic asset, American Jewish elites "remembered" The Holocaust.[29] The conventional account is that they did so because, at the time of the June war, they believed Israel to be in mortal danger and were thus gripped by fears of a "second Holocaust." This claim does not withstand scrutiny.

Consider the first Arab–Israeli war. On the eve of independence in 1948, the threat against Palestinian Jews seemed far more ominous. David Ben-Gurion declared that "700,000 Jews" were "pitted against

[28] Noam Chomsky, *The Fateful Triangle* (Boston: 1983), 4.
[29] Elie Wiesel's career illuminates the nexus between The Holocaust and the June war. Although he had already published his memoir of Auschwitz, Wiesel won public acclaim only after writing two volumes celebrating Israel's victory. (Wiesel, *And the Sea*, 16)

27 million Arabs – one against forty." The United States joined a UN arms embargo on the region, solidifying a clear edge in weaponry enjoyed by the Arab armies. Fears of another Nazi Final Solution haunted American Jewry. Deploring that the Arab states were now "arming Hitler's henchman, the Mufti, while the United States was enforcing its arms embargo," the AJC anticipated "mass suicide and a complete holocaust in Palestine." Even Secretary of State George Marshall and the CIA openly predicted certain Jewish defeat in the event of war.[30] Although the "stronger side, in fact, won" (historian Benny Morris), it was not a walkover for Israel. During the first months of the war, in early 1948, and especially as independence was declared in May, Israel's chances for survival were put at "fifty-fifty" by Yigael Yadin, Haganah chief of operations. Without a secret Czech arms deal, Israel would likely not have survived.[31] After fighting for a year, Israel suffered 6,000 casualties, one percent of its population. Why, then, did The Holocaust not become a focus of American Jewish life after the 1948 war?

Israel quickly proved to be far less vulnerable in 1967 than in its independence struggle. Israeli and American leaders knew beforehand that Israel would easily prevail in a war with the Arab states. This reality became strikingly obvious as Israel routed its Arab neighbors in a few days. As Novick reports, "There were surprisingly few explicit references to the Holocaust in American Jewish mobilization

---

[30] Kaufman, *Ambiguous Partnership*, 287, 306–7. Steven L. Spiegel, *The Other Arab–Israeli Conflict* (Chicago: 1985), 17, 32.

[31] Benny Morris, *1948 And After* (Oxford: 1990), 14–15. Uri Bialer, *Between East and West* (Cambridge: 1990), 180–1.

on behalf of Israel before the war."[32] The Holocaust industry sprung up only *after* Israel's overwhelming display of military dominance and flourished amid extreme Israeli triumphalism.[33] The standard interpretative framework cannot explain these anomalies.

Israel's shocking initial reverses and substantial casualties during, and increasing international isolation after, the October 1973 Arab–Israeli war – conventional accounts maintain – exacerbated American Jewish fears of Israel's vulnerability. Accordingly, Holocaust memory now moved center stage. Novick typically reports: "Among American Jews . . . the situation of a vulnerable and isolated Israel came to be seen as terrifyingly similar to that of European Jewry thirty years earlier. . . . [T]alk of the Holocaust not only 'took off' in America but became increasing [sic] institutionalized."[34] Yet Israel had edged close to the precipice and, in both relative and absolute terms, suffered many more casualties in the 1948 war than in 1973.

True, except for its alliance with the US, Israel was out of favor internationally after the October 1973 war. Compare, however, the 1956 Suez war. Israel and organized American Jewry alleged that, on the eve of the Sinai invasion, Egypt threatened Israel's very existence, and that a full Israeli withdrawal from Sinai would fatally undermine "Israel's vital interests: her survival as a state."[35] The international

[32] Novick, *The Holocaust*, 148.

[33] See, for example, Amnon Kapeliouk, *Israel: la fin des mythes* (Paris: 1975).

[34] Novick, *The Holocaust*, 152.

[35] *Commentary*, "Letter from Israel" (February 1957). Throughout the Suez crisis, *Commentary* repeatedly sounded the warning that Israel's "very survival" was at stake.

community nonetheless stood firm. Recounting his brilliant perform-ance at the UN General Assembly, Abba Eban ruefully recalled, however, that "having applauded the speech with sustained and vigorous applause, it had gone on to vote against us by a huge majority."[36] The United States figured prominently in this consensus. Not only did Eisenhower force Israel's withdrawal, but US public support for Israel fell into "frightening decline" (historian Peter Grose).[37] By contrast, immediately after the 1973 war, the United States provided Israel with massive military assistance, much greater than it had in the preceding four years combined, while American public opinion firmly backed Israel.[38] This was the occasion when "talk of the Holocaust . . . 'took off' in America," at a time when Israel was less isolated than it had been in 1956.

In fact, the Holocaust industry did not move center stage be-cause Israel's unexpected setbacks during, and pariah status following, the October 1973 war prompted memories of the Final Solution. Rather, Sadat's impressive military showing in the October war convinced US and Israeli policy elites that a diplomatic settlement with Egypt, including the return of Egyptian lands seized in June 1967, could no longer be avoided. To increase Israel's negotiating leverage the Holocaust industry increased production quotas. The crucial point is that after the 1973 war Israel was not isolated from the United States: these developments occurred within the framework of the US–Israeli alliance, which remained fully intact.[39] The historical

[36] Abba Eban, *Personal Witness* (New York: 1992), 272.

[37] Peter Grose, *Israel in the Mind of America* (New York: 1983), 304.

[38] A.F.K. Organski, *The $36 Billion Bargain* (New York: 1990), 163, 48.

[39] Finkelstein, *Image and Reality*, chap. 6.

record strongly suggests that, if Israel had truly been alone after the
October war, American Jewish elites would no more have remembered the Nazi holocaust than they did after the 1948 or 1956
war.

Novick provides ancillary explanations that are even less convinc-
ing. Quoting religious Jewish scholars, for example, he suggests that
"the Six Day War offered a folk theology of 'Holocaust and Redemption.'" The "light" of the June 1967 victory redeemed the "darkness"
of the Nazi genocide: "it had given God a second chance." The
Holocaust could emerge in American life only after June 1967 because
"the extermination of European Jewry attained [an] – if not happy, at
least viable – ending." Yet in standard Jewish accounts, not the June
war but Israel's founding marked redemption. Why did The Holocaust
have to await a *second* redemption? Novick maintains that the "image
of Jews as military heroes" in the June war "worked to efface the
stereotype of weak and passive victims which . . . previously inhibited
Jewish discussion of the Holocaust."[40] Yet for sheer courage, the 1948
war was Israel's finest hour. And Moshe Dayan's "daring" and
"brilliant" 100-hour Sinai campaign in 1956 prefigured the swift
victory in June 1967. Why, then, did American Jewry require the
June war to "efface the stereotype"?

Novick's account of how American Jewish elites came to instru-
mentalize the Nazi holocaust is not persuasive. Consider these representative passages:

---

[40] Novick, *The Holocaust*, 149–50. Novick cites here the noted Jewish scholar
Jacob Neusner.

As American Jewish leaders sought to understand the reasons for Israel's isolation and vulnerability – reasons that might suggest a remedy – the explanation commanding the widest support was that the fading of the memories of Nazism's crimes against the Jews, and the arrival on the scene of a generation ignorant of the Holocaust, had resulted in Israel's losing the support it had once enjoyed.

[W]hile American Jewish organizations could do nothing to alter the recent past in the Middle East, and precious little to affect its future, they *could* work to revive memories of the Holocaust. So the "fading memories" explanation offered an agenda for action. [emphasis in original][41]

Why did the "fading memories" explanation for Israel's post-1967 predicament "command[] the widest support"? Surely this was an improbable explanation. As Novick himself copiously documents, the support Israel initially garnered had little to do with "memories of Nazism's crimes,"[42] and, anyhow, these memories had faded long before Israel lost international support. Why could Jewish elites do "precious little to affect" Israel's future? Surely they controlled a formidable organizational network. Why was "reviv[ing] memories of the Holocaust" the only agenda for action? Why not support the international consensus that called for Israel's withdrawal from the lands occupied in the June war *as well as* a "just and lasting peace" between Israel and its Arab neighbors (UN Resolution 242)?

---

[41] Ibid., 153, 155.
[42] Ibid., 69–77.

A more coherent, if less charitable, explanation is that American Jewish elites remembered the Nazi holocaust before June 1967 only when it was politically expedient. Israel, their new patron, had capitalized on the Nazi holocaust during the Eichmann trial.[43] Given its proven utility, organized American Jewry exploited the Nazi holocaust after the June war. Once ideologically recast, The Holocaust (capitalized as I have previously noted) proved to be the perfect weapon for deflecting criticism of Israel. Exactly how I will illustrate presently. What deserves emphasis here, however, is that for American Jewish elites The Holocaust performed the same function as Israel: another invaluable chip in a high-stakes power game. The avowed concern for Holocaust memory was as contrived as the avowed concern for Israel's fate.[44] Thus, organized American Jewry quickly forgave and forgot Ronald Reagan's demented 1985 declaration at Bitburg cemetery that the German soldiers (including Waffen SS members) buried there were "victims of the Nazis just as surely as the victims in the concentration camps." In 1988, Reagan was honored with the "Humanitarian of the Year" award by one of the most prominent Holocaust institutions, the Simon Wiesenthal Center, for his "staunch support of Israel," and in 1994 with the "Torch of Liberty" award by the pro-Israel ADL.[45]

---

[43] Tom Segev, *The Seventh Million* (New York: 1993), part VI.

[44] Concern for survivors of the Nazi holocaust was equally contrived: a liability before June 1967, they were silenced; an asset after June 1967, they were sanctified.

[45] *Response* (December 1988). Prominent Holocaust-mongers and Israel-supporters like ADL national director Abraham Foxman, past president of the AJC Morris Abram, and chairman of the Conference of Presidents of Major

The Reverend Jesse Jackson's earlier outburst in 1979 that he was "sick and tired of hearing about the Holocaust" was not so quickly forgiven or forgotten, however. Indeed, the attacks by American Jewish elites on Jackson never let up, although not for his "anti-Semitic remarks" but rather for his "espousal of the Palestinian position" (Seymour Martin Lipset and Earl Raab).[46] In Jackson's case, an additional factor was at work: he represented domestic constituencies with which organized American Jewry had been at loggerheads since the late 1960s. In these conflicts, too, The Holocaust proved to be a potent ideological weapon.

It was not Israel's alleged weakness and isolation, not the fear of a "second Holocaust," but rather its proven strength and strategic alliance with the United States that led Jewish elites to gear up the Holocaust industry after June 1967. However unwittingly, Novick provides the best evidence to support that conclusion. To prove that power considerations, not the Nazi Final Solution, determined American policy toward Israel, he writes: "It was when the Holocaust was freshest in the mind of American leaders — the first twenty-five years after the end of the war — that the United States was *least* supportive

---

American Jewish Organizations Kenneth Bialkin, not to mention Henry Kissinger, all rose to Reagan's defense during the Bitburg visit, while the AJC hosted West German Chancellor Helmut Kohl's loyal foreign minister as the guest of honor at its annual meeting the same week. In like spirit, Michael Berenbaum of the Washington Holocaust Memorial Museum later attributed Reagan's Bitburg trip and statements to "the naive sense of American optimism." (Shafir, *Ambiguous Relations*, 302–4; Berenbaum, *After Tragedy*, 14)

[46] Seymour Martin Lipset and Earl Raab, *Jews and the New American Scene* (Cambridge: 1995), 159.

of Israel. . . . It was not when Israel was perceived as weak and vulnerable, but after it demonstrated its strength, in the Six Day War, that American aid to Israel changed from a trickle to a flood" (emphasis in original).[47] That argument applies with equal force to American Jewish elites.

~

There are also domestic sources of the Holocaust industry. Mainstream interpretations point to the recent emergence of "identity politics," on the one hand, and the "culture of victimization," on the other. In effect, each identity was grounded in a particular history of oppression; Jews accordingly sought their own ethnic identity in the Holocaust.

Yet, among groups decrying their victimization, including Blacks, Latinos, Native Americans, women, gays and lesbians, Jews alone are not disadvantaged in American society. In fact, identity politics and The Holocaust have taken hold among American Jews not because of victim status but because they are *not* victims.

As anti-Semitic barriers quickly fell away after World War II, Jews rose to preeminence in the United States. According to Lipset and Raab, per capita Jewish income is almost double that of non-Jews; sixteen of the forty wealthiest Americans are Jews; 40 percent of American Nobel Prize winners in science and economics are Jewish, as are 20 percent of professors at major universities; and 40 percent of partners in the leading law firms in New York and Washington.

---

[47] Novick, *The Holocaust*, 166.

The list goes on.[48] Far from constituting an obstacle to success, Jewish identity has become the crown of that success. Just as many Jews kept Israel at arm's length when it constituted a liability and became born-again Zionists when it constituted an asset, so they kept their ethnic identity at arm's length when it constituted a liability and became born-again Jews when it constituted an asset.

Indeed, the secular success story of American Jewry validated a core — perhaps the sole — tenet of their newly acquired identity as Jews. Who could any longer dispute that Jews were a "chosen" people? In *A Certain People: American Jews and Their Lives Today*, Charles Silberman — himself a born-again Jew — typically gushes: "Jews would have been less than human had they eschewed any notion of superiority altogether," and "it is extraordinarily difficult for American Jews to expunge the sense of superiority altogether, however much they may try to suppress it." What an American Jewish child inherits, according to novelist Philip Roth, is "no body of law, no body of learning and no language, and finally, no Lord . . . but a kind of psychology: and the psychology can be translated in three words: 'Jews are better.' "[49] As will be seen presently, The Holocaust was the negative version of their vaunted worldly success: it served to validate Jewish chosenness.

By the 1970s, anti-Semitism was no longer a salient feature of American life. Nonetheless, Jewish leaders started sounding alarm bells that American Jewry was threatened by a virulent "new anti-

[48] Lipset and Raab, *Jews*, 26–7.
[49] Charles Silberman, *A Certain People* (New York: 1985), 78, 80, 81.

Semitism."[50] The main exhibits of a prominent ADL study ("for those who have died because they were Jews") included the Broadway show *Jesus Christ Superstar* and a counterculture tabloid that "portrayed Kissinger as a fawning sycophant, coward, bully, flatterer, tyrant, social climber, evil manipulator, insecure snob, unprincipled seeker after power" – in the event, an understatement.[51]

For organized American Jewry, this contrived hysteria over a new anti-Semitism served multiple purposes. It boosted Israel's stock as the refuge of last resort if and when American Jews needed one. Moreover, the fund-raising appeals of Jewish organizations purportedly combating anti-Semitism fell on more receptive ears. "The anti-Semite is in the unhappy position," Sartre once observed, "of having a vital need for the very enemy he wishes to destroy."[52] For these Jewish organizations the reverse is equally true. With anti-Semitism in short supply, a cutthroat rivalry between major Jewish "defense" organizations – in particular, the ADL and the Simon Wiesenthal Center – has erupted in recent years.[53] In the matter of fund-raising, incidentally, the alleged threats confronting Israel serve a similar purpose. Returning from a trip to the United States, the respected Israeli journalist Danny Rubinstein reported: "According to most of

[50]   Novick, *The Holocaust*, 170–2.

[51]   Arnold Forster and Benjamin R. Epstein, *The New Anti-Semitism* (New York: 1974), 107.

[52]   Jean-Paul Sartre, *Anti-Semite and Jew* (New York: 1965), 28.

[53]   Saidel, *Never Too Late*, 222. Seth Mnookin, "Will NYPD Look to Los Angeles For Latest 'Sensitivity' Training?" in *Forward* (7 January 2000). The article reports that the ADL and Simon Wiesenthal Center are vying for the franchise on programs teaching "tolerance."

the people in the Jewish establishment the important thing is to stress again and again the external dangers that face Israel. . . . The Jewish establishment in America needs Israel only as a victim of cruel Arab attack. For such an Israel one can get support, donors, money. . . . Everybody knows the official tally of the contributions collected in the United Jewish Appeal in America, where the name of Israel is used and about half of the sum goes not to Israel but to the Jewish institutions in America. Is there a greater cynicism?" As we will see, the Holocaust industry's exploitation of "needy Holocaust victims" is the latest and, arguably, ugliest manifestation of this cynicism.[54]

The main ulterior motive for sounding the anti-Semitism alarm bells, however, lay elsewhere. As American Jews enjoyed greater secular success, they moved steadily to the right politically. Although still left-of-center on cultural questions such as sexual morality and abortion, Jews grew increasingly conservative on politics and the economy.[55] Complementing the rightward turn was an inward turn, as Jews, no longer mindful of past allies among the have-nots, increasingly earmarked their resources for Jewish concerns only. This reorientation of American Jewry[56] was clearly evident in growing

[54] Noam Chomsky, *Pirates and Emperors* (New York: 1986), 29–30 (Rubinstein).

[55] For a survey of recent poll data confirming this trend, see Murray Friedman, "Are American Jews Moving to the Right?" in *Commentary* (April 2000). In the 1997 New York City mayoral contest pitting Ruth Messinger, a mainstream Democrat, against Rudolph Giuliani, a law-and-order Republican, for example, fully 75% of the Jewish vote went for Giuliani. Significantly, to vote for Giuliani, Jews had to cross traditional party as well as ethnic lines (Messinger is Jewish).

[56] It seems that the shift was also in part due to the displacement of a cosmopolitan Central European Jewish leadership by arriviste and shtetl-

tensions between Jews and Blacks. Traditionally aligned with black people against caste discrimination in the United States, many Jews broke with the Civil Rights alliance in the late 1960s when, as Jonathan Kaufman reports, "the goals of the civil rights movement were shifting – from demands for political and legal equality to demands for economic equality." "When the civil rights movement moved north, into the neighborhoods of these liberal Jews," Cheryl Greenberg similarly recalls, "the question of integration took on a different tone. With concerns now couched in class rather than racial terms, Jews fled to the suburbs almost as quickly as white Christians to avoid what they perceived as the deterioration of their schools and neighborhoods." The memorable climax was the protracted 1968 New York City teachers' strike, which pitted a largely Jewish professional union against Black community activists fighting for control of failing schools. Accounts of the strike often refer to fringe anti-Semitism. The eruption of Jewish racism – not far below the surface before the strike – is less often remembered. More recently, Jewish publicists and organizations have figured prominently in efforts to dismantle affirmative action programs. In key Supreme Court tests – *DeFunis* (1974) and *Bakke* (1978) – the AJC, ADL, and AJ Congress, apparently reflecting mainstream Jewish sentiment, all filed amicus briefs opposing affirmative action.[57]

---

chauvinist Jews of Eastern European descent like New York City mayor Edward Koch and *New York Times* executive editor A.M. Rosenthal. In this regard it bears notice that the Jewish historians dissenting from Holocaust dogmatism have typically come from Central Europe – for example, Hannah Arendt, Henry Friedlander, Raul Hilberg, and Arno Mayer.

[57] See, e.g., Jack Salzman and Cornel West (eds), *Struggles in the Promised Land*

Moving aggressively to defend their corporate and class interests, Jewish elites branded all opposition to their new conservative policies anti-Semitic. Thus ADL head Nathan Perlmutter maintained that the "real anti-Semitism" in America consisted of policy initiatives "corrosive of Jewish interests," such as affirmative action, cuts in the defense budget, and neo-isolationism, as well as opposition to nuclear power and even Electoral College reform.[58]

In this ideological offensive, The Holocaust came to play a critical role. Most obviously, evoking historic persecution deflected present-day criticism. Jews could even gesture to the "quota system" from which they suffered in the past as a pretext for opposing affirmative action programs. Beyond this, however, the Holocaust framework apprehended anti-Semitism as a strictly irrational Gentile loathing of Jews. It precluded the possibility that animus toward Jews might be grounded in a real conflict of interests (more on this later). Invoking The Holocaust was therefore a ploy to delegitimize all criticism of Jews: such criticism could only spring from pathological hatred.

Just as organized Jewry remembered The Holocaust when Israeli power peaked, so it remembered The Holocaust when American Jewish power peaked. The pretense, however, was that, there and here, Jews faced an imminent "second Holocaust." Thus American Jewish elites could strike heroic poses as they indulged in cowardly bullying. Norman Podhoretz, for example, pointed up the new Jewish

---

(New York: 1997), esp. chaps 6, 8, 9, 14, 15. (Kaufman at 111; Greenberg at 166) To be sure, a vocal minority of Jews dissented from this rightward drift.

[58] Nathan Perlmutter and Ruth Ann Perlmutter, *The Real Anti-Semitism in America* (New York: 1982).

resolve after the June 1967 war to "resist any who would in any way and to any degree and for any reason whatsoever attempt to do us harm. . . . We would from now on stand our ground."[59] Just as Israelis, armed to the teeth by the United States, courageously put unruly Palestinians in their place, so American Jews courageously put unruly Blacks in their place.

Lording it over those least able to defend themselves: that is the real content of organized American Jewry's reclaimed courage.

[59] Novick, *The Holocaust*, 173 (Podhoretz).

CHAPTER 2

HOAXERS, HUCKSTERS, AND HISTORY

"**H**olocaust awareness," the respected Israeli writer Boas Evron observes, is actually "an official, propagandistic indoctrination, a churning out of slogans and a false view of the world, the real aim of which is not at all an understanding of the past, but a manipulation of the present." In and of itself, the Nazi holocaust does not serve any particular political agenda. It can just as easily motivate dissent from as support for Israeli policy. Refracted through an ideological prism, however, "the memory of the Nazi extermination" came to serve – in Evron's words – "as a powerful tool in the hands of the Israeli leadership and Jews abroad."[1] The Nazi holocaust became The Holocaust.

Two central dogmas underpin the Holocaust framework: (1) The Holocaust marks a categorically unique historical event; (2) The Holocaust marks the climax of an irrational, eternal Gentile hatred of

[1] Boas Evron, "Holocaust: The Uses of Disaster," in *Radical America* (July–August 1983), 15.

Jews. Neither of these dogmas figured at all in public discourse before the June 1967 war; and, although they became the centerpieces of Holocaust literature, neither figures at all in genuine scholarship on the Nazi holocaust.[2] On the other hand, both dogmas draw on important strands in Judaism and Zionism.

In the aftermath of World War II, the Nazi holocaust was not cast as a uniquely Jewish – let alone a historically unique – event. Organized American Jewry in particular was at pains to place it in a universalist context. After the June war, however, the Nazi Final Solution was radically reframed. "The first and most important claim that emerged from the 1967 war and became emblematic of American Judaism," Jacob Neusner recalls, was that "the Holocaust . . . was unique, without parallel in human history."[3] In an illuminating essay, historian David Stannard ridicules the "small industry of Holocaust hagiographers arguing for the uniqueness of the Jewish experience with all the energy and ingenuity of theological zealots."[4] The uniqueness dogma, after all, makes no sense.

At the most basic level, every historical event is unique, if merely by virtue of time and location, and every historical event bears distinctive features as well as features in common with other historical events. The anomaly of The Holocaust is that its uniqueness is held to be absolutely decisive. What other historical event, one

[2] For the distinction between Holocaust literature and Nazi holocaust scholarship, see Finkelstein and Birn, *Nation*, part one, section 3.

[3] Jacob Neusner (ed.), *Judaism in Cold War America, 1945–1990*, v. ii: *In the Aftermath of the Holocaust* (New York: 1993), viii.

[4] David Stannard, "Uniqueness as Denial," in Alan Rosenbaum (ed.), *Is the Holocaust Unique?* (Boulder: 1996), 193.

might ask, is framed largely for its categorical uniqueness? Typically, distinctive features of The Holocaust are isolated in order to place the event in a category altogether apart. It is never clear, however, why the many common features should be reckoned trivial by comparison.

All Holocaust writers agree that The Holocaust is unique, but few, if any, agree why. Each time an argument for Holocaust uniqueness is empirically refuted, a new argument is adduced in its stead. The results, according to Jean-Michel Chaumont, are multiple, conflicting arguments that annul each other: "Knowledge does not accumulate. Rather, to improve on the former argument, each new one starts from zero."[5] Put otherwise: uniqueness is a given in the Holocaust framework; proving it is the appointed task, and disproving it is equivalent to Holocaust denial. Perhaps the problem lies with the premise, not the proof. Even if The Holocaust were unique, what difference would it make? How would it change our understanding if the Nazi holocaust were not the first but the fourth or fifth in a line of comparable catastrophes?

The most recent entry into the Holocaust uniqueness sweepstakes is Steven Katz's *The Holocaust in Historical Context*. Citing nearly 5,000 titles in the first of a projected three-volume study, Katz surveys the full sweep of human history in order to prove that "the

---

[5] Jean-Michel Chaumont, *La concurrence des victimes* (Paris: 1997), 148–9. Chaumont's dissection of the "Holocaust uniqueness" debate is a tour de force. Yet his central thesis does not persuade, at least for the American scene. According to Chaumont, the Holocaust phenomenon originated in Jewish survivors' belated search for public recognition of past suffering. Yet survivors hardly figured in the initial push to move The Holocaust center stage.

Holocaust is phenomenologically unique by virtue of the fact that never before has a state set out, as a matter of intentional principle and actualized policy, to annihilate physically every man, woman and child belonging to a specific people." Clarifying his thesis, Katz explains: "φ is uniquely C. φ may share A, B. D, . . . X with ▲ but not C. And again φ may share A, B, D, . . . X with all ▲ but not C. Everything essential turns, as it were, on φ being uniquely C . . . π lacking C is not φ. . . . By definition, no exceptions to this rule are allowed. ▲ sharing A, B, D, . . . X with φ may be like φ in these and other respects . . . but as regards our definition of uniqueness any or all ▲ lacking C are not φ. . . . Of course, in its totality φ is more than C, but it is never φ without C." Translation: A historical event containing a distinct feature is a distinct historical event. To avoid any confusion, Katz further elucidates that he uses the term *phenomenologically* "in a non-Husserlian, non-Shutzean, non-Schelerian, non-Heideggerian, non-Merleau-Pontyan sense." Translation: The Katz enterprise is phenomenal non-sense.[6] Even if the evidence sustained Katz's central thesis, which it does not, it would only prove that The Holocaust contained a distinct feature. The wonder would be were it otherwise. Chaumont infers that Katz's study is actually "ideology" masquerading as "science," more on which presently.[7]

Only a flea's hop separates the claim of Holocaust uniqueness from the claim that The Holocaust cannot be rationally apprehended. If The Holocaust is unprecedented in history, it must stand above and hence cannot be grasped by history. Indeed, The Holocaust is

---

[6] Steven T. Katz, *The Holocaust in Historical Context* (Oxford: 1994), 28, 58, 60.

[7] Chaumont, *La concurrence*, 137.

unique because it is inexplicable, and it is inexplicable because it is unique.

Dubbed by Novick the "sacralization of the Holocaust," this mystifications's most practiced purveyor is Elie Wiesel. For Wiesel, Novick rightly observes, The Holocaust is effectively a "mystery" religion. Thus Wiesel intones that the Holocaust "leads into darkness," "negates all answers," "lies outside, if not beyond, history," "defies both knowledge and description," "cannot be explained nor visualized," is "never to be comprehended or transmitted," marks a "destruction of history" and a "mutation on a cosmic scale." Only the survivor-priest (read: only Wiesel) is qualified to divine its mystery. And yet, The Holocaust's mystery, Wiesel avows, is "noncommunicable"; "we cannot even talk about it." Thus, for his standard fee of $25,000 (plus chauffeured limousine), Wiesel lectures that the "secret" of Auschwitz's "truth lies in silence."[8]

Rationally comprehending The Holocaust amounts, in this view, to denying it. For rationality denies The Holocaust's uniqueness and mystery. And to compare The Holocaust with the sufferings of others constitutes, for Wiesel, a "total betrayal of Jewish history."[9] Some years back, the parody of a New York tabloid was headlined: "Michael Jackson, 60 Million Others, Die in Nuclear Holocaust." The letters

[8] Novick, *The Holocaust*, 200–1, 211–12. Wiesel, *Against Silence*, v. i, 158, 211, 239, 272, v. ii, 62, 81, 111, 278, 293, 347, 371, v. iii, 153, 243. Elie Wiesel, *All Rivers Run to the Sea* (New York: 1995), 89. Information on Wiesel's lecture fee provided by Ruth Wheat of the Bnai Brith Lecture Bureau."Words," according to Wiesel, "are a kind of horizontal approach, while silence offers you a vertical approach. You plunge into it." Does Wiesel parachute into his lectures?

[9] Wiesel, *Against Silence*, v. iii, 146.

46   THE HOLOCAUST INDUSTRY

page carried an irate protest from Wiesel: "How dare people refer to
what happened yesterday as a Holocaust? There was only one
Holocaust. . . ." In his new memoir Wiesel, proving that life can also
imitate spoof, reprimands Shimon Peres for speaking "without hesita-
tion of 'the two holocausts' of the twentieth century: Auschwitz and
Hiroshima. He shouldn't have."[10] A favorite Wiesel tag line declares
that "the universality of the Holocaust lies in its uniqueness."[11] But if

[10] Wiesel, *And the Sea*, 95. Compare these news items:

> Ken Livingstone, a former member of the Labour Party who is running for
> mayor of London as an independent, has incensed Jews in Britain by saying
> global capitalism has claimed as many victims as World War II. "Every year the
> international financial system kills more people than World War II, but at least
> Hitler was mad, you know?" . . . "It's an insult to all those murdered and
> persecuted by Adolf Hitler," said John Butterfill, a Conservative Member of
> Parliament. Mr. Butterfill also said Mr. Livingstone's indictment of the global
> financial system had decidedly anti-Semitic overtones. ("Livingstone's Words
> Anger Jews," in *International Herald Tribune*, 13 April 2000)

> Cuban President Fidel Castro . . . accused the capitalist system of regularly
> causing deaths on the scale of World War II by ignoring the needs of the poor.
> "The images we see of mothers and children in whole regions of Africa under
> the lash of drought and other catastrophes remind us of the concentration
> camps of Nazi Germany." Referring to war crimes trials after World War II,
> the Cuban leader said: "We lack a Nuremberg to judge the economic order
> imposed upon us, where every three years more men, women and children die
> of hunger and preventable diseases than died in the Second World War." . . .
> In New York City, Abraham Foxman, national director of the Anti-Defamation
> League, said . . . "Poverty is serious, it's painful and maybe deadly, but it's not
> the Holocaust and it's not concentration camps." (John Rice, "Castro Viciously
> Attacks Capitalism," in *Associated Press*, 13 April 2000)

[11] Wiesel, *Against Silence*, v. iii, 156, 160, 163, 177.

it is incomparably and incomprehensibly unique, how can The Holocaust have a universal dimension?

The Holocaust uniqueness debate is sterile. Indeed, the claims of
Holocaust uniqueness have come to constitute a form of "intellectual
terrorism" (Chaumont). Those practicing the normal comparative
procedures of scholarly inquiry must first enter a thousand and one
caveats to ward off the accusation of "trivializing The Holocaust."[12]

A subtext of the Holocaust uniqueness claim is that The Holocaust
was uniquely evil. However terrible, the suffering of others simply
does not compare. Proponents of Holocaust uniqueness typically
disclaim this implication, but such demurrals are disingenuous.[13]

The claims of Holocaust uniqueness are intellectually barren and
morally discreditable, yet they persist. The question is, Why? In the
first place, unique suffering confers unique entitlement. The unique
evil of the Holocaust, according to Jacob Neusner, not only sets Jews
apart from others, but also gives Jews a "claim upon those others."

---

[12] Chaumont, *La concurrence*, 156. Chaumont also makes the telling point that
the claim of The Holocaust's incomprehensible evil cannot be reconciled with
the attendant claim that its perpetrators were perfectly normal. (310)

[13] Katz, *The Holocaust*, 19, 22. "The claim that the assertion of the Holocaust's
uniqueness is *not* a form of invidious comparison produces systematic double-
talk," Novick observes. "Does anyone . . . believe that the claim of uniqueness
is anything *other* than a claim for preeminence?" (emphasis in original)
Lamentably, Novick himself indulges such invidious comparing. Thus he
maintains that although morally evasive in an American context, "the repeated
assertion that whatever the United States has done to blacks, Native Americans, Vietnamese, or others pales in comparison to the Holocaust is true."
(*The Holocaust*, 197, 15)

For Edward Alexander, the uniqueness of The Holocaust is "moral capital"; Jews must "claim sovereignty" over this "valuable property."[14]

In effect, Holocaust uniqueness — this "claim" upon others, this "moral capital" — serves as Israel's prize alibi. "The singularity of the Jewish suffering," historian Peter Baldwin suggests, "adds to the moral and emotional claims that Israel can make . . . on other nations."[15] Thus, according to Nathan Glazer, The Holocaust, which pointed to the "peculiar *distinctiveness* of the Jews," gave Jews "the right to consider themselves specially threatened and specially worthy of whatever efforts were necessary for survival."[16] (emphasis in original) To cite one typical example, every account of Israel's decision to develop nuclear weapons evokes the specter of The Holocaust.[17] As if Israel otherwise would not have gone nuclear.

There is another factor at work. The claim of Holocaust uniqueness is a claim of Jewish uniqueness. Not the suffering of Jews but that *Jews* suffered is what made The Holocaust unique. Or: The Holocaust is special because Jews are special. Thus Ismar Schorsch, chancellor of the Jewish Theological Seminary, ridicules the Holocaust uniqueness claim as "a distasteful secular version of chosenness."[18] Vehement as

[14] Jacob Neusner, "A 'Holocaust' Primer," 178. Edward Alexander, "Stealing the Holocaust," 15–16, in Neusner, *Aftermath*.
[15] Peter Baldwin (ed.), *Reworking the Past* (Boston: 1990), 21.
[16] Nathan Glazer, *American Judaism*, second edition (Chicago: 1972), 171.
[17] Seymour M. Hersh, *The Samson Option* (New York: 1991), 22. Avner Cohen, *Israel and the Bomb* (New York: 1998), 10, 122, 342.
[18] Ismar Schorsch, "The Holocaust and Jewish Survival," in *Midstream* (January 1981), 39. Chaumont convincingly demonstrates that the claim of Holocaust uniqueness originated in, and only makes coherent sense in the context of, the religious dogma of Jewish chosenness. *La concurrence*, 102–7, 121.

he is about the uniqueness of The Holocaust, Elie Wiesel is no less vehement that Jews are unique. "Everything about us is different." Jews are "ontologically" exceptional.[19] Marking the climax of a millennial Gentile hatred of Jews, The Holocaust attested not only to the unique suffering of Jews but to Jewish uniqueness as well.

During and in the aftermath of World War II, Novick reports, "hardly anyone inside [the US] government – and hardly anyone outside it, Jew or Gentile – would have understood the phrase 'abandonment of the Jews.'" A reversal set in after June 1967. "The world's silence," "the world's indifference," "the abandonment of the Jews": these themes became a staple of "Holocaust discourse."[20]

Appropriating a Zionist tenet, the Holocaust framework cast Hitler's Final Solution as the climax of a millennial Gentile hatred of Jews. The Jews perished because all Gentiles, be it as perpetrators or as passive collaborators, wanted them dead. "The free and 'civilized' world," according to Wiesel, handed the Jews "over to the executioner. There were the killers – the murderers – and there were those who remained silent."[21] The historical evidence for a murderous Gentile impulse is nil. Daniel Goldhagen's ponderous effort to prove one variant of this claim in *Hitler's Willing Executioners* barely rose to the comical.[22] Its political utility, however, is considerable. One might note, incidentally, that the "eternal anti-Semitism" theory in fact gives comfort to the anti-Semite. As Arendt says in *The Origins of*

---

[19] Wiesel, *Against Silence*, v. i, 153. Wiesel, *And the Sea*, 133.

[20] Novick, *The Holocaust*, 59, 158–9.

[21] Wiesel, *And the Sea*, 68.

[22] Daniel Jonah Goldhagen, *Hitler's Willing Executioners* (New York: 1996). For a critique, see Finkelstein and Birn, *Nation*.

Totalitarianism, "that this doctrine was adopted by professional anti-semites is a matter of course; it gives the best possible alibi for all horrors. If it is true that mankind has insisted on murdering Jews for more than two thousand years, then Jew-killing is a normal, and even human, occupation and Jew-hatred is justified beyond the need of argument. The more surprising aspect of this explanation is that it has been adopted by a great many unbiased historians and by an even greater number of Jews."[23]

The Holocaust dogma of eternal Gentile hatred has served both to justify the necessity of a Jewish state and to account for the hostility directed at Israel. The Jewish state is the only safeguard against the next (inevitable) outbreak of homicidal anti-Semitism; conversely, homicidal anti-Semitism is behind every attack or even defensive maneuver against the Jewish state. To account for criticism of Israel, fiction writer Cynthia Ozick had a ready answer: "The world wants to wipe out the Jews . . . the world has always wanted to wipe out the Jews."[24] If all the world wants the Jews dead, truly the wonder is that they are still alive – and, unlike much of humanity, not exactly starving.

This dogma has also conferred total license on Israel: Intent as the Gentiles always are on murdering Jews, Jews have every right to protect themselves, however they see fit. Whatever expedient Jews might resort to, even aggression and torture, constitutes legitimate self-defense. Deploring the "Holocaust lesson" of eternal Gentile

[23] Hannah Arendt, *The Origins of Totalitarianism* (New York: 1951), 7.
[24] Cynthia Ozick, "All the World Wants the Jews Dead," in *Esquire* (November 1974).

hatred, Boas Evron observes that it "is really tantamount to a deliberate breeding of paranoia. . . . This mentality . . . condones in advance any inhuman treatment of non-Jews, for the prevailing mythology is that 'all people collaborated with the Nazis in the destruction of Jewry,' hence everything is permissible to Jews in their relationship to other peoples."[25]

In the Holocaust framework, Gentile anti-Semitism is not only ineradicable but also always irrational. Going far beyond classical Zionist, let alone standard scholarly, analyses, Goldhagen construes anti-Semitism as "divorced from actual Jews," "fundamentally *not* a response to any objective evaluation of Jewish action," and "independent of Jews' nature and actions." A Gentile mental pathology, its "host domain" is "the mind." (emphasis in original) Driven by "irrational arguments," the anti-Semite, according to Wiesel, "simply resents the fact that the Jew exists."[26] "Not only does anything Jews do or refrain from doing have nothing to do with anti-Semitism," sociologist John Murray Cuddihy critically observes, "but any *attempt* to explain anti-Semitism by referring to the Jewish contribution to anti-Semitism is itself an instance of anti-Semitism!" (emphasis in original)[27] The point, of course, is not that anti-Semitism is justifiable,

---

[25] Boas Evron, *Jewish State or Israeli Nation* (Bloomington: 1995), 226–7.

[26] Goldhagen, *Hitler's Willing Executioners*, 34–5, 39, 42. Wiesel, *And the Sea*, 48.

[27] John Murray Cuddihy, "The Elephant and the Angels: The Incivil Irritatingness of Jewish Theodicy," in Robert N. Bellah and Frederick E. Greenspahn (eds), *Uncivil Religion* (New York: 1987), 24. In addition to this article, see his "The Holocaust: The Latent Issue in the Uniqueness Debate," in P.F. Gallagher (ed.), *Christians, Jews, and Other Worlds* (Highland Lakes, NJ: 1987).

nor that Jews are to blame for crimes committed against them, but that anti-Semitism develops in a specific historical context with its attendant interplay of interests. "A gifted, well-organized, and largely successful minority can inspire conflicts that derive from objective inter-group tensions," Ismar Schorsch points out, although these conflicts are "often packaged in anti-Semitic stereotypes."[28]

The irrational essence of Gentile anti-Semitism is inferred inductively from the irrational essence of The Holocaust. To wit, Hitler's Final Solution uniquely lacked rationality – it was "evil for its own sake," "purposeless" mass killing; Hitler's Final Solution marked the culmination of Gentile anti-Semitism; therefore Gentile anti-Semitism is essentially irrational. Taken apart or together, these propositions do not withstand even superficial scrutiny.[29] Politically, however, the argument is highly serviceable.

By conferring total blamelessness on Jews, the Holocaust dogma immunizes Israel and American Jewry from legitimate censure. Arab

---

[28] Schorsch, *The Holocaust*, 39. Incidentally, the claim that Jews constitute a "gifted" minority is also, in my view, a "distasteful secular version of chosenness."

[29] Whereas a full exposition of this topic is beyond the scope of the essay, consider just the first proposition. Hitler's war against the Jews, even if irrational (and that itself is a complex issue), would hardly constitute a unique historical occurrence. Recall, for example, the central thesis of Joseph Schumpeter's treatise on imperialism that "non-rational and irrational, purely instinctual inclinations toward war and conquest play a very large role in the history of mankind . . . numberless wars – perhaps the majority of all wars – have been waged without . . . reasoned and reasonable interest." (Joseph Schumpeter, "The Sociology of Imperialism," in Paul Sweezy (ed.), *Imperialism and Social Classes* [New York: 1951], 83)

hostility, African-American hostility: they are "fundamentally *not* a response to any objective evaluation of Jewish action" (Goldhagen).[30] Consider Wiesel on Jewish persecution: "For two thousand years . . . we were always threatened. . . . For what? For no reason." On Arab hostility to Israel: "Because of who we are and what our homeland Israel represents – the heart of our lives, the dream of our dreams – when our enemies try to destroy us, they will do so by trying to destroy Israel." On Black people's hostility to American Jews: "The people who take their inspiration from us do not thank us but attack us. We find ourselves in a very dangerous situation. We are again the scapegoat on all sides. . . . We helped the blacks; we always helped them. . . . I feel sorry for blacks. There is one thing they should learn from us and that is gratitude. No people in the world knows gratitude as we do; we are forever grateful."[31] Ever chastised, ever innocent: this is the burden of being a Jew.[32]

---

[30] Explicitly eschewing the Holocaust framework, Albert S. Lindemann's recent study of anti-Semitism starts from the premise that "whatever the power of myth, not all hostility to Jews, individually or collectively, has been based on fantastic or chimerical visions of them, or on projections unrelated to any palpable reality. As human beings, Jews have been as capable as any other group of provoking hostility in the everyday secular world." (*Esau's Tears* [Cambridge: 1997], xvii)

[31] Wiesel, *Against Silence*, v. i, 255, 384.

[32] Chaumont makes the telling point that this Holocaust dogma effectively renders other crimes more acceptable. Insistence on the Jews' radical innocence – i.e. the absence of any rational motive for persecuting, let alone killing, them – "presupposes a 'normal' status for persecutions and killings in other circumstances, creating a de facto division between unconditionally intolerable crimes and crimes which one must – and hence can – live with." (*La concurrence*, 176)

The Holocaust dogma of eternal Gentile hatred also validates the complementary Holocaust dogma of uniqueness. If The Holocaust marked the climax of a millennial Gentile hatred of the Jews, the persecution of non-Jews in The Holocaust was merely accidental and the persecution of non-Jews in history merely episodic. From every standpoint, then, Jewish suffering during The Holocaust was unique.

Finally, Jewish suffering was unique because the Jews are unique. The Holocaust was unique because it was not rational. Ultimately, its impetus was a most irrational, if all-too-human, passion. The Gentile world hated Jews because of envy, jealousy: *ressentiment*. Anti-Semitism, according to Nathan and Ruth Ann Perlmutter, sprang from "gentile jealousy and resentment of the Jews' besting Christians in the marketplace . . . large numbers of less accomplished gentiles resent smaller numbers of more accomplished Jews."[33] Albeit negatively, The Holocaust thus confirmed the chosenness of Jews. Because Jews are better, or more successful, they suffered the ire of Gentiles, who then murdered them.

In a brief aside, Novick muses "what would talk of the Holocaust be like in America" if Elie Wiesel were not its "principal interpreter"?[34] The answer is not difficult to find: Before June 1967 the universalist message of concentration camp survivor Bruno Bettelheim resonated among American Jews. After the June war, Bettelheim was shunted aside in favor of Wiesel. Wiesel's prominence is a function of his ideological utility. Uniqueness of Jewish suffering/uniqueness of the Jews, ever-guilty Gentiles/ever-innocent Jews, unconditional

---

[33] Perlmutters, *Anti-Semitism*, 36, 40.

[34] Novick, *The Holocaust*, 351n19.

defense of Israel/unconditional defense of Jewish interests: Elie Wiesel *is* The Holocaust.

~

Articulating the key Holocaust dogmas, much of the literature on Hitler's Final Solution is worthless as scholarship. Indeed, the field of Holocaust studies is replete with nonsense, if not sheer fraud. Especially revealing is the cultural milieu that nurtures this Holocaust literature.

The first major Holocaust hoax was *The Painted Bird*, by Polish émigré Jerzy Kosinski.[35] The book was "written in English," Kosinski explained, so that "I could write dispassionately, free from the emotional connotation one's native language always contains." In fact, whatever parts he actually wrote – an unresolved question – were written in Polish. The book was purported to be Kosinski's autobiographical account of his wanderings as a solitary child through rural Poland during World War II. In fact, Kosinski lived with his parents throughout the war. The book's motif is the sadistic sexual tortures perpetrated by the Polish peasantry. Pre-publication readers derided it as a "pornography of violence" and "the product of a mind obsessed with sadomasochistic violence." In fact, Kosinski conjured up almost all the pathological episodes he narrates. The book depicts the Polish peasants he lived with as virulently anti-Semitic. "Beat the Jews," they jeer. "Beat the bastards." In fact, Polish peasants harbored the Kosinski family even though they were fully aware of

---

[35] New York: 1965. I rely on James Park Sloan, *Jerzy Kosinski* (New York: 1996), for background.

their Jewishness and the dire consequences they themselves faced if caught.

In the *New York Times Book Review*, Elie Wiesel acclaimed *The Painted Bird* as "one of the best" indictments of the Nazi era, "written with deep sincerity and sensitivity." Cynthia Ozick later gushed that she "immediately" recognized Kosinski's authenticity as "a Jewish survivor and witness to the Holocaust." Long after Kosinski was exposed as a consummate literary hoaxer, Wiesel continued to heap encomiums on his "remarkable body of work."[36]

The Painted Bird became a basic Holocaust text. It was a best-seller and award-winner, translated into numerous languages, and required reading in high school and college classes. Doing the Holocaust circuit, Kosinski dubbed himself a "cut-rate Elie Wiesel." (Those unable to afford Wiesel's speaking fee – "silence" doesn't come cheap – turned to him.) Finally exposed by an investigative newsweekly,

[36] Elie Wiesel, "Everybody's Victim," in *New York Times Book Review* (31 October 1965). Wiesel, *All Rivers*, 335. The Ozick quote is from Sloan, 304–5. Wiesel's admiration of Kosinski does not surprise. Kosinski wanted to analyze the "new language," Wiesel to "forge a new language," of the Holocaust. For Kosinski, "what lies between episodes is both a comment on and something commented upon by the episode." For Wiesel, "the space between any two words is vaster than the distance between heaven and earth." There's a Polish proverb for such profundity: "From empty to vacuum." Both also liberally sprinkled their ruminations with quotes from Albert Camus, the telltale sign of a charlatan. Recalling that Camus once told him, "I envy you for Auschwitz," Wiesel continues: "Camus could not forgive himself for not knowing that majestic event, that mystery of mysteries." (Wiesel, *All Rivers*, 321; Wiesel, *Against Silence*, v. ii., 133)

Kosinski was still stoutly defended by the *New York Times*, which alleged that he was the victim of a Communist plot.[37]

A more recent fraud, Binjamin Wilkomirski's *Fragments*,[38] borrows promiscuously from the Holocaust kitsch of *The Painted Bird*. Like Kosinski, Wilkomirski portrays himself as a solitary child survivor who becomes mute, winds up in an orphanage and only belatedly discovers that he is Jewish. Like *The Painted Bird*, the chief narrative conceit of *Fragments* is the simple, pared-down voice of a child-naif, also allowing time frames and place names to remain vague. Like *The Painted Bird*, each chapter of *Fragments* climaxes in an orgy of violence. Kosinski represented *The Painted Bird* as "the slow unfreezing of the mind"; Wilkomirski represents *Fragments* as "recovered memory."[39]

[37] Geoffrey Stokes and Eliot Fremont-Smith, "Jerzy Kosinski's Tainted Words," in *Village Voice* (22 June 1982). John Corry, "A Case History: 17 Years of Ideological Attack on a Cultural Target," in *New York Times* (7 November 1982). To his credit, Kosinski did undergo a kind of deathbed conversion. In the few years between his exposure and his suicide, Kosinski deplored the Holocaust industry's exclusion of non-Jewish victims. "Many North American Jews tend to perceive it as Shoah, as an exclusively Jewish disaster. . . . But at least half of the world's Romanies (unfairly called Gypsies), some 2.5 million Polish Catholics, millions of Soviet citizens and various nationalities, were also victims of this genocide. . . ." He also paid tribute to the "bravery of the Poles" who "sheltered" him "during the Holocaust" despite his so-called Semitic "looks." (Jerzy Kosinski, *Passing By* [New York: 1992], 165–6, 178–9) Angrily asked at a Holocaust conference what the Poles did to save Jews, Kosinski snapped back: "What did the Jews do to save the Poles?"

[38] New York: 1996. For background to the Wilkomirski hoax, see esp. Elena Lappin, "The Man With Two Heads," in *Granta*, no. 66, and Philip Gourevitch, "Stealing the Holocaust," in *New Yorker* (14 June 1999).

[39] Another important "literary" influence on Wilkomirski is Wiesel. Compare

A hoax cut out of whole cloth, *Fragments* is nevertheless the archetypal Holocaust memoir. It is set first in the concentration camps, where every guard is a crazed, sadistic monster joyfully cracking the skulls of Jewish newborns. Yet, the classic memoirs of the Nazi concentration camps concur with Auschwitz survivor Dr. Ella Lingens-Reiner: "There were few sadists. Not more than five or

---

these passages:

> Wilkomirski: "I saw her wide-open eyes, and all of a sudden I knew: these eyes knew it all, they'd seen everything mine had, they knew infinitely more than anyone else in this country. I knew eyes like this, I'd seen them a thousand times, in the camp and later on. They were Mila's eyes. We children used to tell each other everything with these eyes. She knew it, too; she looked straight through my eyes and into my heart."

> Wiesel: "The eyes – I must tell you about their eyes. I must begin with that, for their eyes precede all else, and everything is comprehended within them. The rest can wait. It will only confirm what you already know. But their eyes – their eyes flame with a kind of irreducible truth, which burns and is not consumed. Shamed into silence before them, you can only bow your head and accept the judgment. Your only wish now is to see the world as they do. A grown man, a man of wisdom and experience, you are suddenly impotent and terribly impoverished. Those eyes remind you of your childhood, your orphan state, cause you to lose all faith in the power of language. Those eyes negate the value of words; they dispose of the need for speech." (*The Jews of Silence* [New York: 1966], 3)

Wiesel rhapsodizes for another page and a half about "the eyes." His literary prowess is matched by his mastery of the dialectic. In one place Wiesel avows, "I believe in collective guilt, unlike many liberals." In another place he avows, "I emphasize that I do not believe in collective guilt." (Wiesel, *Against Silence*, v. ii, 134; Wiesel, *And the Sea*, 152, 235) ten percent."[40] Ubiquitous German sadism figures prominently, however, in Holocaust literature. Doing double service, it "documents" the unique irrationality of The Holocaust as well as the fanatical anti-Semitism of the perpetrators.

The singularity of *Fragments* lies in its depiction of life not during but after The Holocaust. Adopted by a Swiss family, little Binjamin endures yet new torments. He is trapped in a world of Holocaust deniers. "Forget it – it's a bad dream," his mother screams. "It was only a bad dream. . . . You're not to think about it any more." "Here in this country," he chafes, "everyone keeps saying I'm to forget, and that it never happened, I only dreamed it. But they know all about it!"

Even at school, "the boys point at me and make fists and yell: 'He's raving, there's no such thing. Liar! He's crazy, mad, he's an idiot.'" (An aside: They were right.) Pummeling him, chanting anti-Semitic ditties, all the Gentile children line up against poor Binjamin, while the adults keep taunting, "You're making it up!"

Driven to abject despair, Binjamin reaches a Holocaust epiphany. "The camp's still there – just hidden and well disguised. They've taken off their uniforms and dressed themselves up in nice clothes so as not to be recognized. . . . Just give them the gentlest of hints that maybe, possibly, you're a Jew – and you'll feel it: these are the same people, and I'm sure of it. They can still kill, even out of uniform." More than a homage to Holocaust dogma, *Fragments* is the smoking

[40] Bernd Naumann, *Auschwitz* (New York: 1966), 91. See Finkelstein and Birn, *Nation*, 67–8, for extensive documentation.

gun: even in Switzerland – neutral Switzerland – all the Gentiles want to kill the Jews.

Fragments was widely hailed as a classic of Holocaust literature. It was translated into a dozen languages and won the Jewish National Book Award, the *Jewish Quarterly* Prize, and the Prix de Mémoire de la Shoah. Star of documentaries, keynoter at Holocaust conferences and seminars, fund-raiser for the United States Holocaust Memorial Museum, Wilkomirski quickly became a Holocaust poster boy.

Acclaiming *Fragments* a "small masterpiece," Daniel Goldhagen was Wilkomirski's main academic champion. Knowledgeable historians like Raul Hilberg, however, early on pegged *Fragments* as a fraud. Hilberg also posed the right questions after the fraud's exposure: "How did this book pass as a memoir in several publishing houses? How could it have brought Mr. Wilkomirski invitations to the United States Holocaust Memorial Museum as well as recognized universities? How come we have no decent quality control when it comes to evaluating Holocaust material for publication?"[41]

Half-fruitcake, half-mountebank, Wilkomirski, it turns out, spent the entire war in Switzerland. He is not even Jewish. Listen, however, to the Holocaust industry post-mortems:

Arthur Samuelson (publisher): *Fragments* "is a pretty cool book. . . . It's only a fraud if you call it non-fiction. I would then reissue it, in the fiction category. Maybe it's not true – then he's a better writer!"

[41] Lappin, 49. Hilberg always asked the right questions. Hence his pariah status in the Holocaust community; see Hilberg, *The Politics of Memory*, passim.

Carol Brown Janeway (editor and translator): "If the charges . . . turn out to be correct, then what's at issue are not empirical facts that can be checked, but spiritual facts that must be pondered. What would be required is soul-checking, and that's an impossibility."

There's more. Israel Gutman is a director of Yad Vashem and a Holocaust lecturer at Hebrew University. He is also a former inmate of Auschwitz. According to Gutman, "it's not that important" whether *Fragments* is a fraud. "Wilkomirski has written a story which he has experienced deeply; that's for sure. . . . He is not a fake. He is someone who lives this story very deeply in his soul. The pain is authentic." So it doesn't matter whether he spent the war in a concentration camp or a Swiss chalet; Wilkomirski is not a fake if his "pain is authentic": thus speaks an Auschwitz survivor turned Holocaust expert. The others deserve contempt; Gutman, just pity.

The New Yorker titled its exposé of the Wilkomirski fraud "Stealing the Holocaust." Yesterday Wilkomirski was feted for his tales of Gentile evil; today he is chastised as yet another evil Gentile. It's *always* the Gentiles' fault. True, Wilkomirski fabricated his Holocaust past, but the larger truth is that the Holocaust industry, built on a fraudulent misappropriation of history for ideological purposes, was primed to celebrate the Wilkomirski fabrication. He was a Holocaust "survivor" waiting to be discovered.

In October 1999, Wilkomirski's German publisher, withdrawing *Fragments* from bookstores, finally acknowledged publicly that he wasn't a Jewish orphan but a Swiss-born man named Bruno Doessekker. Informed that the jig was up, Wilkomirski thundered defiantly,

"I am Binjamin Wilkomirski!" Not until a month later did the American publisher, Schocken, drop *Fragments* from its list.[42]

Consider now Holocaust secondary literature. A telltale sign of this literature is the space given over to the "Arab connection." Although the Mufti of Jerusalem didn't play "any significant part in the Holocaust," Novick reports, the four-volume *Encyclopedia of the Holocaust* (edited by Israel Gutman) gave him a "starring role." The Mufti also gets top billing in Yad Vashem: "The visitor is left to conclude," Tom Segev writes, "that there is much in common between the Nazis' plans to destroy the Jews and the Arabs' enmity to Israel." At an Auschwitz commemoration officiated by clergy representing all religious denominations, Wiesel objected *only* to the presence of a Muslim qadi: "Were we not forgetting . . . Mufti Hajj Amin el-Husseini of Jerusalem, Heinrich Himmler's friend?" Incidentally, if the Mufti figured so centrally in Hitler's Final Solution, the wonder is that Israel didn't bring him to justice like Eichmann. He was living openly right next door in Lebanon after the war.[43]

Especially in the wake of Israel's ill-fated invasion of Lebanon in 1982 and as official Israeli propaganda claims came under withering attack by Israel's "new historians," apologists desperately sought to tar the Arabs with Nazism. Famed historian Bernard Lewis managed to devote a full chapter of his short history of anti-Semitism, and fully three pages of his "brief history of the last 2,000 years" of the Middle

[42] "Publisher Drops Holocaust Book," in *New York Times* (3 November 1999). Allan Hall and Laura Williams, "Holocaust Hoaxer?" in *New York Post* (4 November 1999).

[43] Novick, *The Holocaust*, 158. Segev, *Seventh Million*, 425. Wiesel, *And the Sea*, 198.

East, to Arab Nazism. At the liberal extreme of the Holocaust spectrum, Michael Berenbaum of the Washington Holocaust Memorial Museum generously allowed that "the stones thrown by Palestinian youths angered by Israel's presence . . . are not synonymous with the Nazi assault against powerless Jewish civilians."[44]

The most recent Holocaust extravaganza is Daniel Jonah Gold-hagen's *Hitler's Willing Executioners*. Every important journal of opinion printed one or more reviews within weeks of its release. *The New York Times* featured multiple notices, acclaiming Goldhagen's book as "one of those rare new works that merit the appellation landmark" (Richard Bernstein). With sales of half a million copies and translations slated for 13 languages, *Hitler's Willing Executioners* was hailed in *Time* magazine as the "most talked about" and second best nonfiction book of the year.[45]

Pointing to the "remarkable research," and "wealth of proof . . . with overwhelming support of documents and facts," Elie Wiesel heralded *Hitler's Willing Executioners* as a "tremendous contribution to the understanding and teaching of the Holocaust." Israel Gutman praised it for "raising anew clearly central questions" that "the main body of Holocaust scholarship" ignored. Nominated for the Holocaust chair at Harvard University, paired with Wiesel in the national media, Goldhagen quickly became a ubiquitous presence on the Holocaust circuit.

---

[44] Bernard Lewis, *Semites and Anti-Semites* (New York: 1986), chap. 6; Bernard Lewis, *The Middle East* (New York: 1995), 348–50. Berenbaum, *After Tragedy*, 84.

[45] *New York Times*, 27 March, 2 April, 3 April 1996. *Time*, 23 December 1996.

The central thesis of Goldhagen's book is standard Holocaust dogma: driven by pathological hatred, the German people leapt at the opportunity Hitler availed them to murder the Jews. Even leading Holocaust writer Yehuda Bauer, a lecturer at the Hebrew University and director of Yad Vashem, has at times embraced this dogma. Reflecting several years ago on the perpetrators' mindset, Bauer wrote: "The Jews were murdered by people who, to a large degree, did not actually hate them. . . . The Germans did not have to hate the Jews in order to kill them." Yet, in a recent review of Goldhagen's book, Bauer maintained the exact opposite: "The most radical type of murderous attitudes dominated from the end of the 1930s onward. . . . [B]y the outbreak of World War II the vast majority of Germans had identified with the regime and its antisemitic policies to such an extent that it was easy to recruit the murderers." Questioned about this discrepancy, Bauer replied: "I cannot see any contradiction between these statements."[46]

Although bearing the apparatus of an academic study, *Hitler's Willing Executioners* amounts to little more than a compendium of sadistic violence. Small wonder that Goldhagen vigorously championed Wilkomirski: *Hitler's Willing Executioners* is *Fragments* plus footnotes. Replete with gross misrepresentations of source material and internal contradictions, *Hitler's Willing Executioners* is devoid of schol-

---

[46] Yehuda Bauer, "Reflections Concerning Holocaust History," in Louis Greenspan and Graeme Nicholson (eds), *Fackenheim* (Toronto: 1993), 164, 169. Yehuda Bauer, "On Perpetrators of the Holocaust and the Public Discourse," in *Jewish Quarterly Review*, no. 87 (1997), 348–50. Norman G. Finkelstein and Yehuda Bauer, "Goldhagen's *Hitler's Willing Executioners*: An Exchange of Views," in *Jewish Quarterly Review*, nos 1–2 (1998), 126.

arly value. In *A Nation on Trial*, Ruth Bettina Birn and this writer documented the shoddiness of Goldhagen's enterprise. The ensuing controversy instructively illuminated the inner workings of the Holocaust industry.

Birn, the world's leading authority on the archives Goldhagen consulted, first published her critical findings in the Cambridge *Historical Journal*. Refusing the journal's invitation for a full rebuttal, Goldhagen instead enlisted a high-powered London law firm to sue Birn and Cambridge University Press for "many serious libels." Demanding an apology, a retraction, and a promise from Birn that she not repeat her criticisms, Goldhagen's lawyers then threatened that "the generation of any publicity on your part as a result of this letter would amount to a further aggravation of damages."[47]

Soon after this writer's equally critical findings were published in *New Left Review*, Metropolitan, an imprint of Henry Holt, agreed to publish both essays as a book. In a front-page story, the *Forward* warned that Metropolitan was "preparing to bring out a book by Norman Finkelstein, a notorious ideological opponent of the State of Israel." The *Forward* acts as the main enforcer of "Holocaust correctness" in the United States.

Alleging that "Finkelstein's glaring bias and audacious statements . . . are irreversibly tainted by his anti-Zionist stance," ADL head

---

[47] For background and the next paragraphs, see Charles Glass, "Hitler's (un)willing executioners," in *New Statesman* (23 January 1998), Laura Shapiro, "A Battle Over the Holocaust," in *Newsweek* (23 March 1998), and Tibor Krausz, "The Goldhagen Wars," in *Jerusalem Report* (3 August 1998). For these and related items, cf. *www.NormanFinkelstein.com* (with a link to Goldhagen's web site).

Abraham Foxman called on Holt to drop publication of the book: "The issue . . . is not whether Goldhagen's thesis is right or wrong but what is 'legitimate criticism' and what goes beyond the pale." "Whether Goldhagen's thesis is right or wrong," Metropolitan associate publisher Sara Bershtel replied, "is precisely the issue."

Leon Wieseltier, literary editor of the pro-Israel *New Republic*, intervened personally with Holt president Michael Naumann. "You don't know who Finkelstein is. He's poison, he's a disgusting self-hating Jew, he's something you find under a rock." Pronouncing Holt's decision a "disgrace," Elan Steinberg, executive director of the World Jewish Congress, opined, "If they want to be garbagemen they should wear sanitation uniforms."

"I have never experienced," Naumann later recalled, "a similar attempt of interested parties to publicly cast a shadow over an upcoming publication." The prominent Israeli historian and journalist, Tom Segev, observed in *Haaretz* that the campaign verged on "cultural terrorism."

As chief historian of the War Crimes and Crimes Against Humanity Section of the Canadian Department of Justice, Birn next came under attack from Canadian Jewish organizations. Claiming that I was "anathema to the vast majority of Jews on this continent," the Canadian Jewish Congress denounced Birn's collaboration in the book. Exerting pressure through her employer, the CJC filed a protest with the Justice Department. This complaint, joined to a CJC-backed report calling Birn "a member of the perpetrator race" (she is German-born), prompted an official investigation of her.

Even after the book's publication, the ad hominem assaults did not let up. Goldhagen alleged that Birn, who has made the prosecution of

Nazi war criminals her life's work, was a purveyor of anti-Semitism, and that I was of the opinion that Nazism's victims, including my own family, deserved to die.[48] Goldhagen's colleagues at the Harvard Center for European Studies, Stanley Hoffmann and Charles Maier, publicly lined up behind him.[49]

Calling the charges of censorship a "canard," *The New Republic* maintained that "there is a difference between censorship and upholding standards." *A Nation on Trial* received endorsements from the leading historians on the Nazi holocaust, including Raul Hilberg, Christopher Browning and Ian Kershaw. These same scholars uniformly dismissed Goldhagen's book; Hilberg called it "worthless." Standards, indeed.

Consider, finally, the pattern: Wiesel and Gutman supported Goldhagen; Wiesel supported Kosinski; Gutman and Goldhagen supported Wilkomirski. Connect the players: this is Holocaust literature.

[48] Daniel Jonah Goldhagen, "Daniel Jonah Goldhagen Comments on Birn," in *German Politics and Society* (Summer 1998), 88, 91n2. Daniel Jonah Goldhagen, "The New Discourse of Avoidance," n25 (*www.Goldhagen.com/nda2html*)

[49] Hoffmann was Goldhagen's advisor for the dissertation that became *Hitler's Willing Executioners*. Yet, in an egregious breach of academic protocol, he not only wrote a glowing review of Goldhagen's book for *Foreign Affairs* but also denounced *A Nation on Trial* as "shocking" in a second review for the same journal. (*Foreign Affairs*, May/June 1996 and July/August 1998) Maier posted a lengthy intervention on the H-German web site (*www2.h-net.msu.edu*). Ultimately, the only "aspects of this unfolding situation" that Maier found "really distasteful and reprehensible" were the criticisms of Goldhagen. Thus he lent "support to a subsequent finding of malice" in Goldhagen's lawsuit against Birn and deplored my argumentation as "fanciful and inflammatory speculation." (23 November 1997)

All the hype notwithstanding, there is no evidence that Holocaust deniers exert any more influence in the United States than the flat-earth society does. Given the nonsense churned out daily by the Holocaust industry, the wonder is that there are so *few* skeptics. The motive behind the claim of widespread Holocaust denial is not hard to find. In a society saturated with The Holocaust, how else to justify yet more museums, books, curricula, films and programs than to conjure up the bogy of Holocaust denial? Thus Deborah Lipstadt's acclaimed book, *Denying the Holocaust*,[50] as well as the results of an ineptly worded American Jewish Committee poll alleging pervasive Holocaust denial,[51] were released just as the Washington Holocaust Memorial Museum opened.

Denying the Holocaust is an updated version of the "new anti-

---

[50] New York: 1994. Lipstadt occupies the Holocaust chair at Emory University and was recently appointed to the United States Holocaust Memorial Council.

[51] Employing a double negative, the AJC poll practically invited confusion: "Does it seem possible or does it seem impossible to you that the Nazi extermination of the Jews never happened?" Twenty-two percent of respondents answered "It seems possible." In subsequent polls, which rephrased the question straightforwardly, Holocaust denial approached zero. A recent AJC survey of 11 countries found that, notwithstanding pervasive right-wing extremists' claims to the contrary, "few people denied the Holocaust." (Jennifer Golub and Renae Cohen, *What Do Americans Know About the Holocaust?* [The American Jewish Committee: 1993]; "Holocaust Deniers Unconvincing – Surveys," in *Jerusalem Post* [4 February 2000]) Yet in Congressional testimony regarding "anti-Semitism in Europe," David Harris of the AJC highlighted the salience of Holocaust denial in the European Right without once mentioning the AJC's own finding that this denial finds virtually no resonance among the general public. (Hearings before the Foreign Relations Committee, United States Senate, 5 April 2000)

Semitism" tracts. To document widespread Holocaust denial, Lipstadt cites a handful of crank publications. Her *pièce de résistance* is Arthur Butz, a nonentity who teaches electrical engineering at Northwestern University and who published his book *The Hoax of the Twentieth Century* with an obscure press. Lipstadt entitles the chapter on him "Entering the Mainstream." Were it not for the likes of Lipstadt, no one would ever have heard of Arthur Butz.

In fact, the one truly mainstream holocaust denier is Bernard Lewis. A French court even convicted Lewis of denying genocide. But Lewis denied the Turkish genocide of Armenians during World War I, not the Nazi genocide of Jews, and Lewis is pro-Israel.[52] Accordingly, this instance of holocaust denial raises no hackles in the United States. Turkey is an Israeli ally, extenuating matters even further. Mention of an Armenian genocide is therefore taboo. Elie Wiesel and Rabbi Arthur Hertzberg as well as the AJC and Yad Vashem withdrew from an international conference on genocide in Tel Aviv because the academic sponsors, against Israeli government urging, included sessions on the Armenian case. Wiesel also sought, unilaterally, to abort the conference and, according to Yehuda Bauer, personally lobbied others not to attend.[53] Acting at Israel's behest,

---

[52] See "France Fines Historian Over Armenian Denial," in *Boston Globe* (22 June 1995), and "Bernard Lewis and the Armenians," in *Counterpunch* (16–31 December 1997).

[53] Israel Charny, "The Conference Crisis. The Turks, Armenians and the Jews," in *The Book of the International Conference on the Holocaust and Genocide. Book One: The Conference Program and Crisis* (Tel Aviv: 1982). Israel Amrani, "A Little Help for Friends," in *Haaretz* (20 April 1990) (Bauer). In Wiesel's bizarre account, he resigned as conference chair in order "not to offend our

the US Holocaust Council practically eliminated mention of the Armenians in the Washington Holocaust Memorial Museum, and Jewish lobbyists in Congress blocked a day of remembrance for the Armenian genocide.[54]

To question a survivor's testimony, to denounce the role of Jewish collaborators, to suggest that Germans suffered during the bombing of Dresden or that any state except Germany committed crimes in World War II — this is all evidence, according to Lipstadt, of Holocaust denial.[55] And to suggest that Wiesel has profited from the Holocaust industry, or even to question him, amounts to Holocaust denial.[56]

The most "insidious" forms of Holocaust denial, Lipstadt suggests, are "immoral equivalencies": that is, denying the uniqueness of The Holocaust.[57] This argument has intriguing implications. Daniel Goldhagen argues that Serbian actions in Kosovo "are, in their essence, different from those of Nazi Germany only in scale."[58] That would make Goldhagen "in essence" a Holocaust denier. Indeed, across the political spectrum, Israeli commentators compared Serbia's actions in

---

Armenian guests." Presumably he also attempted to abort the conference and urged others against attending out of courtesy to the Armenians. (Wiesel, *And the Sea*, 92)

[54] Edward T. Linenthal, *Preserving Memory* (New York: 1995), 228ff., 263, 312–13.

[55] Lipstadt, *Denying*, 6, 12, 22, 89–90.

[56] Wiesel, *All Rivers*, 333, 336.

[57] Lipstadt, *Denying*, chapter 11.

[58] "A New Serbia," in *New Republic* (17 May 1999).

Kosovo with Israeli actions in 1948 against the Palestinians.[59] By Goldhagen's reckoning, then, Israel committed a Holocaust. Not even Palestinians claim that anymore.

Not all revisionist literature – however scurrilous the politics or motivations of its practitioners – is totally useless. Lipstadt brands David Irving "one of the most dangerous spokespersons for Holocaust denial" (he recently lost a libel suit in England against her for these and other assertions). But Irving, notorious as an admirer of Hitler and sympathizer with German national socialism, has nevertheless, as Gordon Craig points out, made an "indispensable" contribution to our knowledge of World War II. Both Arno Mayer, in his important study of the Nazi holocaust, and Raul Hilberg cite Holocaust denial publications. "If these people want to speak, let them," Hilberg observes. "It only leads those of us who do research to re-examine what we might have considered as obvious. And that's useful for us."[60]

~

---

[59] See, for example, Meron Benvenisti, "Seeking Tragedy," in *Haaretz* (16 April 1999), Zeev Chafets, "What Undergraduate Clinton Has Forgotten," in *Jerusalem Report* (10 May 1999), and Gideon Levi, "Kosovo: It is Here," in *Haaretz* (4 April 1999). (Benvenisti limits the Serbian comparison to Israeli actions after May 1948.)

[60] Arno Mayer, *Why Did the Heavens Not Darken?* (New York: 1988). Christopher Hitchens, "Hitler's Ghost," in *Vanity Fair* (June 1996) (Hilberg). For a balanced assessment of Irving, see Gordon A. Craig, "The Devil in the Details," in *New York Review of Books* (19 September 1996). Rightly dismissing Irving's claims on the Nazi holocaust as "obtuse and quickly discredited," Craig nonetheless continues: "He knows more about National Socialism than

Annual Days of Remembrance of the Holocaust are a national event. All 50 states sponsor commemorations, often in state legislative chambers. The Association of Holocaust Organizations lists over 100 Holocaust institutions in the United States. Seven major Holocaust museums dot the American landscape. The centerpiece of this memorialization is the United States Holocaust Memorial Museum in Washington.

The first question is why we even have a federally mandated and funded Holocaust museum in the nation's capitol. Its presence on the Washington Mall is particularly incongruous in the absence of a museum commemorating crimes in the course of American history. Imagine the wailing accusations of hypocrisy here were Germany to build a national museum in Berlin to commemorate not the Nazi genocide but American slavery or the extermination of the Native Americans.[61]

---

most professional scholars in his field, and students of the years 1933–1945 owe more than they are always willing to admit to his energy as a researcher and to the scope and vigor of his publications. . . . His book *Hitler's War* . . . remains the best study we have of the German side of the Second World War and, as such, indispensable for all students of that conflict. . . . Such people as David Irving, then, have an indispensable part in the historical enterprise, and we dare not disregard their views."

[61] For the abortive attempts between 1984 and 1994 to build a national African-American museum on the Washington Mall, see Fath Davis Ruffins, "Culture Wars Won and Lost, Part II: The National African-American Museum Project," in *Radical History Review* (Winter 1998). The Congressional initiative was finally killed by Senator Jesse Helms of North Carolina. The Washington Holocaust museum's annual budget is $50 million, of which $30 million is federally subsidized.

It "tries meticulously to refrain from any attempt at indoctrination," the Holocaust museum's designer wrote, "from any manipulation of impressions or emotions." Yet from conception through completion, the museum was mired in politics.[62] With a reelection campaign looming, Jimmy Carter initiated the project to placate Jewish contributors and voters, galled by the President's recognition of the "legitimate rights" of Palestinians. The chairman of the Conference of Presidents of Major American Jewish Organizations, Rabbi Alexander Schindler, deplored Carter's recognition of Palestinian humanity as a "shocking" initiative. Carter announced plans for the museum while Prime Minister Menachem Begin was visiting Washington and in the midst of a bruising Congressional battle over the Administration's proposed sale of weaponry to Saudi Arabia. Other political issues also emerge in the museum. It mutes the Christian background to European anti-Semitism so as not to offend a powerful constituency. It downplays the discriminatory US immigration quotas before the war, exaggerates the US role in liberating the concentration camps, and silently passes over the massive US recruitment of Nazi war criminals at the war's end. The Museum's overarching message is that "we" couldn't even conceive, let alone commit, such evil deeds. The Holocaust "cuts against the grain of the American ethos," Michael Berenbaum observes in the companion book to the museum. "We see in [its] perpetration a violation of every essential American value." The Holocaust museum signals the Zionist lesson that Israel was the

---

[62] For background, see Linenthal, *Preserving Memory*, Saidel, *Never Too Late*, esp. chaps 7, 15, and Tim Cole, *Selling the Holocaust* (New York: 1999), chap. 6.

"appropriate answer to Nazism" with the closing scenes of Jewish survivors struggling to enter Palestine.[63]

The politicization begins even before one crosses the museum's threshold. It is situated on Raoul Wallenberg Place. Wallenberg, a Swedish diplomat, is honored because he rescued thousands of Jews and ended up in a Soviet prison. Fellow Swede Count Folke Bernadotte is not honored because, although he too rescued thousands of Jews, former Israeli Prime Minister Yitzak Shamir ordered his assassination for being too "pro-Arab."[64]

The crux of Holocaust museum politics, however, bears on *whom* to memorialize. Were Jews the only victims of The Holocaust, or did others who perished because of Nazi persecution also count as

---

[63] Michael Berenbaum, *The World Must Know* (New York: 1993), 2, 214. Omer Bartov, *Murder In Our Midst* (Oxford: 1996), 180.

[64] For details, see Kati Marton, *A Death in Jerusalem* (New York: 1994), chap. 9. In his memoir Wiesel recalls the "legendary 'terrorist' past" of Bernadotte's actual assassin, Yehoshua Cohen. Note the inverted commas around terrorist. (Wiesel, *And the Sea*, 58) The New York City Holocaust Museum, although no less mired in politics (both Mayor Ed Koch and Governor Mario Cuomo were courting Jewish votes and money), was also from early on a plaything of local Jewish developers and financiers. At one point, developers sought to downplay "Holocaust" in the museum's name for fear that it would depress property values in the adjacent luxury housing complex. Wags quipped that the complex should be named "Treblinka Towers," and the surrounding streets "Auschwitz Avenue" and "Birkenau Boulevard." The museum solicited funds from J. Peter Grace despite revelations of his association with a convicted Nazi war criminal, and it organized a gala at The Hot Rod – "The New York Holocaust Memorial Commission invites you to Rock and Roll the Night Away." (Saidel, *Never Too Late*, 8, 121, 132, 145, 158, 161, 191, 240)

victims?[65] During the museum's planning stages, Elie Wiesel (along with Yehuda Bauer of Yad Vashem) led the offensive to commemorate Jews alone. Deferred to as the "undisputed expert on the Holocaust period," Wiesel tenaciously argued for the preeminence of Jewish victimhood. "As always, they began with Jews," he typically intoned. "As always, they did not stop with Jews alone."[66] Yet not Jews but Communists were the first political victims, and not Jews but the handicapped were the first genocidal victims, of Nazism.[67]

Justifying preemption of the Gypsy genocide posed the main challenge to the Holocaust Museum. The Nazis systematically

---

[65] Novick dubs this the "6 million" versus "11 million" controversy. The 5 million figure for non-Jewish civilian deaths apparently originated with famed "Nazi-hunter" Simon Wiesenthal. Noting that it "makes no historical sense," Novick writes, "Five million is either much too low (for all non-Jewish civilians killed by the Third Reich) or much too high (for non-Jewish groups targeted, like Jews, for murder)." He hastens to add, however, that "what's at stake, of course, is not numbers as such, but what we mean, what we're referring to, when we talk of 'the Holocaust.' " Strangely, after entering this caveat, Novick supports commemorating only Jews because the 6 million figure "describes something specific and determinate," while the 11 million figure "is unacceptably mushy." (Novick, The Holocaust, 214–26)

[66] Wiesel, Against Silence, v. iii. 162, 166.

[67] For the handicapped as Nazism's first genocidal victims, see esp. Henry Friedlander, The Origins of Nazi Genocide (Chapel Hill: 1995). According to Leon Wieseltier, the non-Jews who perished at Auschwitz "died a death invented for the Jews . . . victims of a 'solution' designed for others" (Leon Wieseltier, "At Auschwitz Decency Dies Again," in New York Times [3 September 1989]). Yet, as numerous scholarly studies show, it was the death invented for handicapped Germans that was then inflicted on Jews; in addition to Friedlander's study, see, for example, Michael Burleigh, Death and Deliverance (Cambridge: 1994).

murdered as many as a half-million Gypsies, with proportional losses roughly equal to the Jewish genocide.[68] Holocaust writers like Yehuda Bauer maintained that the Gypsies did not fall victim to the same genocidal onslaught as Jews. Respected holocaust historians like Henry Friedlander and Raul Hilberg, however, have argued that they did.[69]

Multiple motives lurked behind the museum's marginalizing of the Gypsy genocide. First: one simply couldn't compare the loss of Gypsy and Jewish life. Ridiculing the call for Gypsy representation on the US Holocaust Memorial Council as "cockamamie," executive director Rabbi Seymour Siegel doubted whether Gypsies even "existed" as a people: "There should be some recognition or acknowledgment of the gypsy people . . . if there is such a thing." He did allow, however, that "there was a suffering element under the Nazis." Edward Linenthal recalls the Gypsy representatives' "deep suspicion" of the council, "fueled by clear evidence that some council members viewed

---

[68] See Guenter Lewy, *The Nazi Persecution of the Gypsies* (Oxford: 2000), 221–2, for various estimates of Gypsies killed.

[69] Friedlander, *Origins*: "Alongside Jews, the Nazis murdered the European Gypsies. Defined as a 'dark-skinned' racial group, Gypsy men, women and children could not escape their fate as victims of Nazi genocide. . . . [T]he Nazi regime systematically murdered only three groups of human beings: the handicapped, Jews, and Gypsies" (xii–xiii). (Apart from being a first-rate historian, Friedlander is also a former Auschwitz inmate.) Raul Hilberg, *The Destruction of the European Jews* (New York: 1985) (in three volumes), v. iii, 999–1000. With his usual veracity, Wiesel claims disappointment in his memoir that the Holocaust Memorial Council, which he chaired, didn't include a Gypsy representative – as if he had been powerless to nominate one. (Wiesel, *And the Sea*, 211)

Rom participation in the museum the way a family deals with unwelcome, embarrassing relatives."[70]

Second: acknowledging the Gypsy genocide meant the loss of an exclusive Jewish franchise over The Holocaust, with a commensurate loss of Jewish "moral capital." Third: if the Nazis persecuted Gypsies and Jews alike, the dogma that The Holocaust marked the climax of a millennial Gentile hatred of Jews was clearly untenable. Likewise, if Gentile envy spurred the Jewish genocide, did envy also spur the Gypsy genocide? In the museum's permanent exhibition, non-Jewish victims of Nazism receive only token recognition.[71]

Finally, the Holocaust museum's political agenda has also been shaped by the Israel–Palestine conflict. Before serving as the museum's director, Walter Reich wrote a paean to Joan Peters's fraudulent *From Time Immemorial*, which claimed that Palestine was literally empty before Zionist colonization.[72] Under State Department pressure, Reich was forced to resign after refusing to invite Yasir Arafat, now a compliant American ally, to visit the museum. Offered a sub-director's position, Holocaust theologian John Roth was then badgered into resigning because of past criticism of Israel. Repudiating a

[70] Linenthal, *Preserving Memory*, 241–6, 315.

[71] Although the New York City Holocaust Museum's "particularistic Jewish bent" (Saidel) was even more pronounced – non-Jewish victims of Nazism early on received notice that it was "for Jews only" – Yehuda Bauer flew into a rage at the Commission's mere hint that the Holocaust encompassed more than Jewish losses. "Unless this is immediately and radically changed," Bauer threatened in a letter to Commission members, "I shall take every opportunity to . . . attack this outrageous design from every public platform I have." (Saidel, *Never Too Late*, 125–6, 129, 212, 221, 224–5)

[72] For background, see Finkelstein, *Image and Reality*, chap. 2.

book the museum originally endorsed because it included a chapter
by Benny Morris, a prominent Israeli historian critical of Israel, Miles
Lerman, the museum's chairman, avowed, "To put this museum on
the opposite side of Israel – it's inconceivable."[73]

In the wake of Israel's appalling attacks against Lebanon in 1996,
climaxing in the massacre of more than a hundred civilians at Qana,
Haaretz columnist Ari Shavit observed that Israel could act with
impunity because "we have the Anti-Defamation League . . . and Yad
Vashem and the Holocaust Museum."[74]

---

[73] "ZOA Criticizes Holocaust Museum's Hiring of Professor Who Compared
Israel to Nazis," in *Israel Wire* (5 June 1998). Neal M. Sher, "Sweep the
Holocaust Museum Clean," in *Jewish World Review* (22 June 1998). "Scoundrel
Time," in *PS – The Intelligent Guide to Jewish Affairs* (21 August 1998). Daniel
Kurtzman, "Holocaust Museum Taps One of Its Own for Top Spot," in *Jewish
Telegraphic Agency* (5 March 1999). Ira Stoll, "Holocaust Museum Acknowl-
edges a Mistake," in *Forward* (13 August 1999).

[74] Noam Chomsky, *World Orders Old and New* (New York: 1996), 293–4 (Shavit).

CHAPTER 3

THE DOUBLE SHAKEDOWN

The term "Holocaust survivor" originally designated those who suffered the unique trauma of the Jewish ghettos, concentration camps and slave labor camps, often in sequence. The figure for these Holocaust survivors at war's end is generally put at some 100,000.[1] The number of living survivors cannot be more than a quarter of this figure now. Because enduring the camps became a crown of martyrdom, many Jews who spent the war elsewhere represented themselves as camp survivors. Another strong motive behind this misrepresentation, however, was material. The postwar German government provided compensation to Jews who had been in ghettos or camps. Many Jews fabricated their pasts to meet this eligibility requirement.[2] "If everyone who claims to be a survivor actually is one," my mother used to exclaim, "who did Hitler kill?"

[1] Henry Friedlander, "Darkness and Dawn in 1945: The Nazis, the Allies, and the Survivors," in *US Holocaust Memorial Museum, 1945 — the Year of Liberation* (Washington: 1995), 11–35.

[2] See, for example, Segev, *Seventh Million*, 248.

Indeed, many scholars have cast doubt on the reliability of survivor testimony. "A great percentage of the mistakes I discovered in my own work," Hilberg recalls, "could be attributed to testimonies." Even within the Holocaust industry, Deborah Lipstadt, for example, wryly observes that Holocaust survivors frequently maintain they were personally examined by Josef Mengele at Auschwitz.[3]

Apart from the frailties of memory, some Holocaust survivor testimony may be suspect for additional reasons. Because survivors are now revered as secular saints, one doesn't dare question them. Preposterous statements pass without comment. Elie Wiesel reminisces in his acclaimed memoir that, recently liberated from Buchenwald and only eighteen years old, "I read *The Critique of Pure Reason* – don't laugh! – in Yiddish." Leaving aside Wiesel's acknowledgment that at the time "I was wholly ignorant of Yiddish grammar," *The Critique of Pure Reason* was never translated into Yiddish. Wiesel also remembers in intricate detail a "mysterious Talmudic scholar" who "mastered Hungarian in two weeks, just to surprise me." Wiesel tells a Jewish weekly that he "often gets hoarse or loses his voice" as he silently reads his books to himself "aloud, inwardly." And to a *New York Times* reporter, he recalls that he was once hit by a taxi in Times Square. "I flew an entire block. I was hit at 45th Street and Broadway, and the ambulance picked me up at 44th." "The truth I present is unvarnished," Wiesel sighs, "I cannot do otherwise."[4]

---

[3] Lappin, *Man With Two Heads*, 48. D.D. Guttenplan, "The Holocaust on Trial," in *Atlantic Monthly* (February 2000), 62 (but cf. text above, where Lipstadt equates doubting a survivor's testimony with Holocaust denial).

[4] Wiesel, *All Rivers*, 121–30, 139, 163–4, 201–2, 336. *Jewish Week*, 17 September 1999. *New York Times*, 5 March 1997.

In recent years, "Holocaust survivor" has been redefined to designate not only those who endured but also those who managed to evade the Nazis. It includes, for example, more than 100,000 Polish Jews who found refuge in the Soviet Union after the Nazi invasion of Poland. However, "those who had lived in Russia had not been treated differently than citizens of the country," historian Leonard Dinnerstein observes, while "the survivors of the concentration camps looked like the living dead."[5] One contributor to a Holocaust web site maintained that, although he spent the war in Tel Aviv, he was a Holocaust survivor because his grandmother died in Auschwitz. To judge by Israel Gutman, Wilkomirski is a Holocaust survivor because his "pain is authentic." The Israeli Prime Minister's office recently put the number of "living Holocaust survivors" at nearly a million. The main motive behind this inflationary revision is again not hard to find. It is difficult to press massive new claims for reparations if only a handful of Holocaust survivors are still alive. In fact, Wilkomirski's main accomplices were, in one way or another, tapped into the Holocaust reparations network. His childhood friend from Auschwitz, "little Laura," collected money from a Swiss Holocaust fund although in reality she was an American-born frequenter of satanic cults. His chief Israeli sponsors were active in or subsidized by organizations involved in Holocaust compensation.[6]

The reparations issue provides unique insight into the Holocaust industry. As we have seen, aligning with the United States in the

---

[5] Leonard Dinnerstein, *America and the Survivors of the Holocaust* (New York: 1982), 24.

[6] Daniel Ganzfried, "Binjamin Wilkomirski und die verwandelte Polin," in *Weltwoche* (4 November 1999).

Cold War, Germany was quickly rehabilitated and the Nazi holocaust forgotten. Nonetheless, in the early 1950s Germany entered into negotiations with Jewish institutions and signed indemnification agreements. With little if any external pressure, it has paid out to date some $60 billion.

Compare first the American record. Some 4–5 million men, women and children died as a result of the US wars in Indochina. After the American withdrawal, a historian recalls, Vietnam desperately needed aid. "In the South, 9,000 out of 15,000 hamlets, 25 million acres of farmland, 12 million acres of forest were destroyed, and 1.5 million farm animals had been killed; there were an estimated 200,000 prostitutes, 879,000 orphans, 181,000 disabled people, and 1 million widows; all six of the industrial cities in the North had been badly damaged, as were provincial and district towns, and 4,000 out of 5,800 agricultural communes." Refusing, however, to pay any reparations, President Carter explained that "the destruction was mutual." Declaring that he saw no need for "any apologies, certainly, for the war itself," President Clinton's Defense Secretary, William Cohen, similarly opined: "Both nations were scarred by this. They have their scars from the war. We certainly have ours."[7]

The German government sought to compensate Jewish victims with three different agreements signed in 1952. Individual claimants received payments according to the terms of the Law on Indemnification (*Bundesentschädigungsgesetz*). A separate agreement with Israel subsidized the absorption and rehabilitation of several hundred thou-

---

[7] Marilyn B. Young, *The Vietnam Wars* (New York: 1991), 301–2. "Cohen: US Not Sorry for Vietnam War," in *Associated Press* (11 March 2000).

sand Jewish refugees. The German government also negotiated at the same time a financial settlement with the Conference on Jewish Material Claims Against Germany, an umbrella of all major Jewish organizations including the American Jewish Committee, American Jewish Congress, Bnai Brith, the Joint Distribution Committee, and so forth. The Claims Conference was supposed to use the monies, $10 million annually for twelve years, or about a billion dollars in current values, for Jewish victims of Nazi persecution who had fallen through the cracks in the compensation process.[8] My mother was a case in point. A survivor of the Warsaw Ghetto, Majdanek concentration camp and slave labor camps at Czestochowa and Skarszysko-Kamiena, she received only $3,500 in compensation from the German government. Other Jewish victims (and many who in fact were not victims), however, received lifetime pensions from Germany eventually totaling hundreds of thousands of dollars. The monies given to the Claims Conference were earmarked for those Jewish victims who had received only minimal compensation.

Indeed, the German government sought to make explicit in the agreement with the Claims Conference that the monies would go solely to Jewish survivors, strictly defined, who had been unfairly or inadequately compensated by German courts. The Conference expressed outrage that its good faith was doubted. After reaching agreement, the Conference issued a press release underlining that the monies would be used for "Jewish persecutees of the Nazi regime for

---

[8] For background, see esp. Nana Sagi, *German Reparations* (New York: 1986), and Ronald W. Zweig, *German Reparations and the Jewish World* (Boulder: 1987). Both volumes are official histories commissioned by the Claims Conference.

whom the existing and proposed legislation cannot provide a remedy." The final accord called on the Conference to use the monies "for the relief, rehabilitation and resettlement of Jewish victims."

The Claims Conference promptly annulled the agreement. In a flagrant breach of its letter and spirit, the Conference earmarked the monies not for the rehabilitation of Jewish victims but rather for the rehabilitation of Jewish *communities*. Indeed, a guiding principle of the Claims Conference prohibited use of monies for "direct allocations to individuals." In a classic instance of looking after one's own, however, the Conference provided exemptions for two categories of victims: rabbis and "outstanding Jewish leaders" received individual payments. The constituent organizations of the Claims Conference used the bulk of the monies to finance various pet projects. Whatever benefits (if any) the actual Jewish victims received were indirect or incidental.[9] Large sums were circuitously channeled to Jewish communities in the Arab world and facilitated Jewish emigration from Eastern Europe.[10]

---

[9] In reply to a question recently put by German Parliament member Martin Hohmann (CDU), the German government acknowledged (albeit in extremely convoluted language) that only about 15 percent of the monies given to the Claims Conference actually benefited Jewish victims of Nazi persecution. (personal communication, 23 February 2000)

[10] In his official history, Ronald Zweig explicitly acknowledges that the Claims Conference violated the agreement's terms: "The influx of Conference funds allowed the Joint [Distribution Committee] to continue programs in Europe it would otherwise have terminated, and to undertake programs it would otherwise not have considered because of lack of funds. But the most significant change in the JDC budget resulting from reparations payments was the allocation for the Moslem countries, where the Joint's activities increased by an average of 68 percent during the first three years of Conference

They also subsidized cultural undertakings such as Holocaust museums and university chairs in Holocaust studies, as well as a Yad Vashem showboat pensioning "righteous Gentiles."

More recently, the Claims Conference sought to appropriate for itself denationalized Jewish properties in the former East Germany worth hundreds of millions of dollars that rightfully belonged to living Jewish heirs. As the Conference came under attack by defrauded Jews for this and other abuses, Rabbi Arthur Hertzberg cast a plague on both sides, sneering that "it's not about justice, it's a fight for money."[11] When Germans or Swiss refuse to pay compensation, the heavens cannot contain the righteous indignation of organized American Jewry. But when Jewish elites rob Jewish survivors, no ethical issues arise: it's just about money.

Although my late mother received only $3,500 in compensation, others involved in the reparations process have made out quite well.

---

allocations. Despite the formal restrictions on the use of the reparation funds in the agreement with Germany, the money was used where the needs were the greatest. Moses Leavitt [senior Claims Conference officer] . . . observed: 'Our budget was based on priority of needs in and outside of Israel, the Moslem countries, all included. . . . We did not consider the Conference fund as anything but a part of a general fund placed at our disposal in order to meet the area of Jewish needs for which we were responsible, the area of greatest priority' " (*German Reparations*, 74).

[11] See for example Lorraine Adams, "The Reckoning," in *Washington Post Magazine* (20 April 1997), Netty C. Gross, "The Old Boys Club," and "After Years of Stonewalling, the Claims Conference Changes Policy," in *Jerusalem Report* (15 May 1997, 16 August 1997), Rebecca Spence, "Holocaust Insurance Team Racking Up Millions in Expenses as Survivors Wait," in *Forward* (30 July 1999), and Verena Dobnik, "Oscar Hammerstein's Cousin Sues German Bank Over Holocaust Assets," in *AP Online* (20 November 1998) (Hertzberg).

The reported annual salary of Saul Kagan, long-time Executive Secretary of the Claims Conference, is $105,000. Between stints at the
Conference, Kagan was convicted of 33 counts of willfully misapplying
funds and credit while heading a New York bank. (The conviction was
overturned only after multiple appeals.) Alfonse D'Amato, the ex-
Senator from New York, mediates Holocaust lawsuits against German
and Austrian banks for $350 per hour plus expenses. For the first 6
months of his labors, he took in $103,000. Earlier Wiesel publicly
praised D'Amato for his "sensitivity to Jewish suffering." Lawrence
Eagleburger, Secretary of State under President Bush, earns an annual
salary of $300,000 as chair of the International Commission On Holo-
caust-Era Insurance Claims. "Whatever he's being paid," Elan Steinberg
of the World Jewish Congress opined, "it is an absolute bargain." Kagan
rings up in 12 days, Eagleburger in 4 days, and D'Amato in 10 hours
what my mother received for suffering six years of Nazi persecution.[12]

The award for most enterprising Holocaust huckster, however,
must surely go to Kenneth Bialkin. For decades a prominent US
Jewish leader, he headed the ADL and chaired the Conference of
Presidents of Major American Jewish Organizations. Currently,
Bialkin represents the Generali insurance company *against* the Eagle-
burger Commission for a reported "high sum of money."[13]

~

[12] Greg B. Smith, "Federal Judge OKs Holocaust Accord," in *Daily News* (7
January 2000). Janny Scott, "Jews Tell of Holocaust Deposits," in *New York
Times* (17 October 1996). Saul Kagan read a draft of this section on the
Claims Conference. The final version incorporates all his factual corrections.
[13] Elli Wohlgelernter, "Lawyers and the Holocaust," in *Jerusalem Post* (6 July 1999).

In recent years, the Holocaust industry has become an outright extortion racket. Purporting to represent all of world Jewry, living and dead, it is laying claim to Holocaust-era Jewish assets throughout Europe. Fittingly dubbed the "last chapter of The Holocaust," this double shakedown of European countries as well as legitimate Jewish claimants first targeted Switzerland. I will first review the allegations against the Swiss. I will then turn to the evidence, demonstrating that many of the charges were not only based on deceit but apply even more accurately to those issuing them than to their targets.

Commemorating the 50th anniversary of the end of World War II, Switzerland's president formally apologized in May 1995 for denying Jews refuge during the Nazi holocaust.[14] About the same time, discussion reopened on the long-simmering question of Jewish assets deposited in Swiss accounts before and during the war. In a widely reported story, an Israeli journalist cited a document – misread, as it turned out – proving that Swiss banks still held Holocaust-era Jewish accounts worth billions of dollars.[15]

The World Jewish Congress, a moribund organization until its campaign denouncing Kurt Waldheim as a war criminal, leapt at this

---

[14] For background to this section, see Tom Bower, *Nazi Gold* (New York: 1998), Itamar Levin, *The Last Deposit* (Westport, Conn.: 1999), Gregg J. Rickman, *Swiss Banks and Jewish Souls* (New Brunswick, NJ: 1999), Isabel Vincent, *Hitler's Silent Partners* (New York: 1997), Jean Ziegler, *The Swiss, the Gold and the Dead* (New York: 1997). Although suffering from a pronounced anti-Swiss bias, these books contain much useful information.

[15] Levin, *Last Deposit*, chaps 6–7. For the erroneous Israeli report (although he doesn't mention it, Levin was the author), see Hans J. Halbheer, "To Our American Friends," in *American Swiss Foundation Occasional Papers* (n.d.).

new opportunity to flex its muscle. Early on it was understood that Switzerland was easy prey. Few would sympathize with rich Swiss bankers as against "needy Holocaust survivors." But more importantly, Swiss banks were highly vulnerable to economic pressures from the United States.[16]

In late 1995, Edgar Bronfman, president of the WJC and the son of a Jewish Claims Conference official, and Rabbi Israel Singer, the secretary-general of the WJC and a real estate tycoon, met with the Swiss bankers.[17] Bronfman, heir to the Seagram liquor fortune (his personal wealth is estimated at $3 billion), would later modestly inform the Senate Banking Committee that he spoke "on behalf of the Jewish people" as well as "the 6 million, those who cannot speak for themselves."[18] The Swiss bankers declared that they could locate only 775 unclaimed dormant accounts, worth a total of $32 million. They

---

[16] Thirteen branches of six Swiss banks operated in the United States. Swiss banks loaned American businesses $38 billion in 1994, and managed hundreds of billions of dollars in investments in American stocks and banks for their clients.

[17] In 1992, the WJC spawned a new organization, the World Jewish Restitution Organization (WJRO), which claimed legal jurisdiction over the assets of Holocaust survivors, living and dead. Headed by Bronfman, the WJRO is formally an umbrella of Jewish organizations modeled on the Jewish Claims Conference.

[18] Hearings before the Committee on Banking, Housing, and Urban Affairs, United States Senate, 23 April 1996. Bronfman's defense of "Jewish interests" is highly selective. He is a major business associate of the right-wing German media mogul Leo Kirch, notorious in recent years for trying to fire a German newspaper editor who supported a Supreme Court decision barring Christian crosses in public schools. (*www.Seagram.com/company_info/history/main.html*; Oliver Gehrs, "Einfluss aus der Dose," in *Tagesspiegel* [12 September 1995])

offered this sum as a basis for negotiations with the WJC, which refused it as inadequate. In December 1995, Bronfman teamed up with Senator D'Amato. His poll ratings at a nadir and a Senate race not far off, D'Amato savored this occasion to boost his standing in the Jewish community, with its crucial votes and wealthy political donors. Before the Swiss were finally brought to their knees, the WJC, working with the gamut of Holocaust institutions (including the US Holocaust Memorial Museum and the Simon Wiesenthal Center), had mobilized the entire US political establishment. From President Clinton, who buried the hatchet with D'Amato (the Whitewater hearings were still going on) to lend support, through eleven agencies of the federal government as well as the House and Senate, down to state and local governments across the country, bipartisan pressures were brought to bear as one public official after another lined up to denounce the perfidious Swiss.

Using the House and Senate banking committees as a springboard, the Holocaust industry orchestrated a shameless campaign of vilification. With an infinitely compliant and credulous press ready to give banner headlines to any Holocaust-related story, however preposterous, the smear campaign proved unstoppable. Gregg Rickman, D'Amato's chief legislative aide, boasts in his account that the Swiss bankers were forced "into the court of public opinion where we controlled the agenda. The bankers were on our turf and conveniently, we were judge, jury, and executioner." Tom Bower, a main researcher in the anti-Swiss campaign, dubs the D'Amato call for hearings a "euphemism for a public trial or a kangaroo court."[19]

---

[19] Rickman, *Swiss Banks*, 50–1. Bower, *Nazi Gold*, 299–300.

The "mouthpiece" of the anti-Swiss juggernaut was WJC executive director Elan Steinberg. His main function was dispensing disinformation. "Terror by embarrassment," according to Bower, "was Steinberg's weapon, as he uttered a string of accusations designed to cause discomfort and shock. OSS reports, often based on rumor and uncorroborated sources and disregarded for years by historians as hearsay, suddenly assumed uncritical credibility and widespread publicity." "The last thing the banks need is negative publicity," Rabbi Singer explained. "We will do it until the banks say, 'Enough. We want a compromise.'" Anxious to share the limelight, Rabbi Marvin Hier, Dean of the Simon Wiesenthal Center, spectacularly alleged that the Swiss incarcerated refugee Jews in "slave-labor camps." (With wife and son on the payroll, Hier runs the Simon Wiesenthal Center as a family business; together the Hiers drew a salary of $520,000 in 1995. The Center is renowned for its "Dachau-meets-Disneyland" museum exhibits and "the successful use of sensationalistic scare tactics for fund-raising.") "In light of the media barrage of mixing truth and assumption, fact and fiction," Itamar Levin concludes, "it is easy to understand why many Swiss believe their country was the victim of an international conspiracy of some kind."[20]

---

[20] Bower, *Nazi Gold*, 295 ("mouthpiece"), 306–7; cf. 319. Alan Morris Schom, "The Unwanted Guests, Swiss Forced Labor Camps, 1940–1944," A Report Prepared for the Simon Wiesenthal Center, January 1998. (Schom states these were "in reality slave-labor camps.") Levin, *Last Deposit*, 158, 188. For a sober treatment of the Swiss refugee camps, see Ken Newman (ed.), *Swiss Wartime Work Camps: A Collection of Eyewitness Testimonies, 1940–1945* (Zurich: 1999), and International Commission of Experts, Switzerland – Second World War, *Switzerland and Refugees in the Nazi Era* (Bern: 1999), chap. 4.4.4. Saidel,

The campaign rapidly degenerated into a libel of the Swiss people. Bower, in a study supported by D'Amato's office and the Simon Wiesenthal Center, typically reports that "a country whose citizens . . . boasted to their neighbors about their enviable wealth, was quite knowingly profiting from blood money"; that "the apparently respectable citizens of the world's most peaceful nation . . . committed an unprecedented theft"; that "dishonesty was a cultural code that individual Swiss had mastered to protect the nation's image and prosperity"; that the Swiss were "instinctively attracted to healthy profits" (only the Swiss?); that "self-interest was the supreme guide for all of Switzerland's banks" (only Switzerland's banks?); that "Switzerland's small breed of bankers had become greedier and more immoral than most"; that "concealment and deception were practiced arts among Swiss diplomats" (only Swiss diplomats?); that "apologies and resignations were not common in Switzerland's political tradition" (unlike our own?); that "Swiss greed was unique"; that the "Swiss character" combined "simplicity and duplicity," and "behind the appearance of civility was a layer of obstinacy, and beyond that was solid egotistical incomprehension of anyone else's opinion"; that the Swiss were "not just a peculiarly charmless people who had produced no artists, no heroes since William Tell and no statesmen, but were dishonest Nazi collaborators who had profited from genocide," and on and on. Rickman points to this "deeper truth" about the Swiss: "Down deep, perhaps deeper than they thought, a latent arrogance about

---

Never Too Late, 222–3 ("Dachau", "sensationalistic"). Yossi Klein Halevi, "Who Owns the Memory?" in *Jerusalem Report* (25 February 1993). Wiesenthal rents out his name to the Center for $90,000 annually.

themselves and against others existed in their very makeup. Try as they did, they could not hide their upbringing."[21] Many of these slurs are remarkably like the slurs cast against Jews by anti-Semites.

The main charge was that there had been, in the words of Bower's subtitle, "a fifty-year Swiss-Nazi conspiracy to steal billions from Europe's Jews and Holocaust survivors." In what has become a mantra of the Holocaust restitution racket, this constituted "the greatest robbery in the history of mankind." For the Holocaust industry, all matters Jewish belong in a separate, superlative category – *the* worst, *the* greatest. . . .

The Holocaust industry first alleged that Swiss banks had systematically denied legitimate heirs of Holocaust victims access to dormant accounts worth between $7 billion and $20 billion. "For the past 50 years," *Time* reported in a cover story, a "standing order" of the Swiss banks "has been to stall and stonewall when Holocaust survivors ask about their dead relatives' accounts." Recalling the secrecy legislation enacted by Swiss banks in 1934 partly to prevent a Nazi shakedown of Jewish depositors, D'Amato lectured the House Banking Committee: "Isn't it ironic that the very system that encouraged people to come and open accounts, the secrecy was then used to deny the people themselves, and their heirs, their legacy, their right? It was perverted, distorted, twisted."

Bower breathlessly recounts the discovery of one key piece of evidence of Swiss perfidy against Holocaust victims: "Luck and diligence provided a nugget that confirmed the validity of Bronfman's

[21] Bower, *Nazi Gold*, xi, xv, 8, 9, 42, 44, 56, 84, 100, 150, 219, 304. Rickman, *Swiss Banks*, 219.

complaint. An intelligence report from Switzerland in July 1945 stated that Jacques Salmanovitz, the owner of the Société Générale de Surveillance, a notary and trust company in Geneva with links to the Balkan countries, possessed a list of 182 Jewish clients who had entrusted 8.4 million Swiss francs and about $90,000 to the notary pending their arrival from the Balkans. The report added that Jews had still not claimed their possessions. Rickman and D'Amato were ecstatic." In his own account, Rickman likewise brandishes this "proof of Swiss criminality." Neither, however, mentions in this specific context that Salmanovitz was Jewish. (The actual validity of these claims will be discussed below.)[22]

In late 1996 a parade of elderly Jewish women and one man delivered moving testimony before the Congressional banking committees on the malfeasance of the Swiss bankers. Yet almost none of these witnesses, according to Itamar Levin, an editor of Israel's main business newspaper, "had real proof of the existence of assets in Swiss banks." To enhance the theatrical effect of this testimony, D'Amato called Elie Wiesel to bear witness. In testimony later widely quoted, Wiesel expressed shock – shock! – at the revelation that the perpetrators of the Holocaust sought to plunder Jews before killing them: "In the beginning we thought the final solution was motivated by poisoned ideology alone. Now we know that they didn't simply want to kill Jews, as horrible as this may sound, they wanted Jewish

---

[22] Thomas Sancton, "A Painful History," in *Time*, 24 February 1997. Hearings before the Committee on Banking and Financial Services, House of Representatives, 25 June 1997. Bower, *Nazi Gold*, 301–2. Rickman, *Swiss Banks*, 48. Levin is equally silent on Salmanovitz being a Jew (cf. 5, 129, 135).

money. Each day we learn more about that tragedy. Is there no limit
to pain? No limit to the outrage?" Of course, Nazi plunder of the
Jews is hardly news; a large part of Raul Hilberg's seminal study, *The
Destruction of the European Jews*, published in 1961, is devoted to the
Nazi expropriation of the Jews.[23]

It was also claimed that the Swiss bankers filched the deposits of
Holocaust victims and methodically destroyed vital records to cover
their tracks, and that only Jews suffered all these abominations.
Assailing the Swiss at one hearing, Senator Barbara Boxer declared:
"This Committee will not stand for two-faced behavior on the part of
the Swiss banks. Don't tell the world that you are searching when
you are shredding."[24]

Alas, the "propaganda value" (Bower) of elderly Jewish claimants
testifying to Swiss perfidy quickly exhausted itself. The Holocaust
industry accordingly sought out a new exposé. The media frenzy
fixed on the Swiss purchase of gold that the Nazis looted from the
central treasuries of Europe during the war. Although billed as a
startling revelation, it was in fact old news. The author of a standard
study on the subject, Arthur Smith, told the House hearing: "I have
listened all morning and this afternoon to things that, to a large
extent, in outline, were known for a number of years; and I am
surprised about the fact that much of it is presented as new and

---

[23] Levin, *Last Deposit*, 60. Hearings before the Committee on Banking and
Financial Services, House of Representatives, 11 December 1996 (quoting
Wiesel's 16 October 1996 Senate Banking Committee testimony). Raul
Hilberg, *The Destruction of the European Jews* (New York: 1961), chap. 5.

[24] Hearings before the Committee on Banking, Housing, and Urban Affairs,
United States Senate, 6 May 1997.

sensational." The point of the hearings, however, was not to inform but, in journalist Isabel Vincent's words, "to create sensational stories." If enough mud was flung, it was reasonably assumed, Switzerland would give in.[25]

The one truly novel allegation was that the Swiss knowingly trafficked in "victim gold." That is, they purchased vast quantities of gold which the Nazis had resmelted into bars after stripping down concentration- and death-camp victims. The WJC, Bower reports, "needed an emotive issue to link the Holocaust and Switzerland." This new revelation of Swiss treachery was accordingly treated as a godsend. "Few images," Bower continues, "were more searing than the methodical extraction in the extermination camps of gold dental fillings from the mouths of Jewish corpses dragged from the gas chambers." "The facts are very, very distressing," D'Amato mournfully intoned at a House hearing, "because they talk about taking and the plundering of assets from homes, from national banks, from the death camps, gold watches and bracelets and eyeglasses frames and the fillings from people's teeth."[26]

Apart from blocking access to Holocaust accounts and purchas-

---

[25] Hearings before the Committee on Banking and Financial Services, House of Representatives, 11 December 1996. Smith complained to the press that the documents he had unearthed long before were being touted by D'Amato as new discoveries. In a bizarre defense, Rickman, who mobilized a massive contingent of researchers through the US Holocaust museum for the Congressional hearings, replies: "While I knew about Smith's book, I made a point of not reading it so that I could not be accused of using 'his' documents" (113). Vincent, *Silent Partners*, 240.

[26] Bower, *Nazi Gold*, 307. Hearings before the Committee on Banking and Financial Services, House of Representatives, 25 June 1997.

ing looted gold, the Swiss also stood accused of conspiring with Poland and Hungary to defraud Jews. The charge was that monies in unclaimed Swiss accounts belonging to Polish and Hungarian nationals (many but not all Jewish) were used by Switzerland as compensation for Swiss properties nationalized by these governments. Rickman refers to this as a "startling revelation, one that would knock the socks off the Swiss and create a firestorm." But the facts were already widely known and reported in American law journals in the early 1950s. And, for all the media ballyhoo, the total sums involved ultimately came to less than a million dollars in current values.[27]

Already prior to the first Senate hearing on the dormant accounts in April 1996, the Swiss banks had agreed to establish an investigative committee and abide by its findings. Composed of six members, three each from the World Jewish Restitution Organization and the Swiss Bankers Association, and headed by Paul Volcker, former chairman of the US Federal Reserve Bank, the "independent committee of eminent persons" was formally charged in a May 1996 "Memorandum of Understanding." In addition, the Swiss government appointed in December 1996 an "independent commission of experts," chaired by Professor Jean-François Bergier and including prominent Israeli holo-

---

[27] Rickman, *Swiss Banks*, 77. For the definitive treatment of this topic, see Peter Hug and Marc Perrenoud, *Assets in Switzerland of Victims of Nazism and the Compensation Agreements with East Bloc Countries* (Bern: 1997). For early discussion in the United States, see Seymour J. Rubin and Abba P. Schwartz, "Refugees and Reparations," in *Law and Contemporary Problems* (Duke University School of Law: 1951), 283.

caust scholar Saul Friedländer, to investigate Switzerland's gold trade with Germany during World War II.

Before these bodies could even commence work, however, the Holocaust industry pressed for a financial settlement with Switzerland. The Swiss protested that any settlement should naturally await the commissions' findings; otherwise, it constituted "extortion and blackmail." Playing its ever-winning card, the WJC anguished over the plight of "needy Holocaust survivors." "My problem is the timing," Bronfman told the House Banking Committee in December 1996, "and I have all of these Holocaust survivors that I am worried about." One wonders why the anguished billionaire couldn't himself temporarily relieve their plight. Dismissing one Swiss settlement offer of $250 million, Bronfman sniffed: "Don't do any favors. I'll give the money myself." He didn't. Switzerland, however, agreed in February 1997 to establish a $200 million "Special Fund for Needy Victims of the Holocaust" to tide over "persons who need help or support in special ways" until the commissions completed their work. (The fund was still solvent when the Bergier and Volcker commissions issued their reports.) The pressures from the Holocaust industry for a final settlement, however, did not relent; rather, they continued to mount. Renewed Swiss pleas that a settlement should await the commissions' findings – it was the WJC, after all, that originally called for this moral reckoning – still fell on deaf ears. In fact, the Holocaust industry stood only to lose from these findings: should just a few claims ultimately prove legitimate, the case against the Swiss banks would lose credibility; and should the legitimate claimants be identified, even if a large number, the Swiss would be obliged to compensate only them, but not the Jewish organizations. Another mantra of the Holocaust industry is that compensation "is about truth and justice, not about money." "It's not about money," the Swiss now quipped. "It's about more money."[28]

Beyond whipping up public hysteria, the Holocaust industry coordinated a two-pronged strategy to "terrorize" (Bower) the Swiss into submission: class-action lawsuits and an economic boycott. The first class-action lawsuit was filed in early October 1996 by Edward Fagan and Robert Swift on behalf of Gizella Weisshaus (her father spoke about monies deposited in Switzerland before his death in Auschwitz, but the banks rebuffed her postwar inquiries) and "others similarly situated" for $20 billion. A few weeks later the Simon Wiesenthal Center, enlisting attorneys Michael Hausfeld and Melvyn Weiss, filed a second class-action lawsuit, and in January 1997 the World Council of Orthodox Jewish Communities initiated yet a third one. All three suits were filed before Judge Edward Korman, a US District Court judge in Brooklyn, who consolidated them. At least one party to the case, Toronto-based attorney Sergio Karas, deplored this tactic: "The class-action suits have done nothing but provoke mass hysteria and Swiss-bashing. They're just perpetuating the myth about Jewish lawyers who just want money." Paul Volcker opposed the class-action

[28] Levin, *Last Deposit*, 93, 186. Hearings before the Committee on Banking and Financial Services, House of Representatives, 11 December 1996. Rickman, *Swiss Banks*, 218. Bower, *Nazi Gold*, 318, 323. A week after establishing the Special Fund, Switzerland's president, "terrified of unremitting hostility in America" (Bower), announced the creation of a $5 billion Solidarity Foundation "to reduce poverty, despair, and violence" globally. The foundation's approval, however, required a national referendum, and domestic opposition quickly surfaced. Its fate remains uncertain.

suits on the grounds that they "will impair our work, potentially to the point of ineffectiveness" – for the Holocaust industry an irrelevant concern, if not an added incentive.[29]

The main weapon used to break Swiss resistance, however, was the economic boycott. "Now the battle will be much dirtier," Avraham Burg, chair of the Jewish Agency and Israel's point man in the Swiss banking case, warned in January 1997. "Until now we have held back international Jewish pressure." Already in January 1996 the WJC had begun plotting the boycott. Bronfman and Singer contacted New York City Comptroller Alan Hevesi (whose father had been a prominent AJC official) and New York State Comptroller Carl McCall. Between them, the two comptrollers invest billions of dollars in pension funds. Hevesi also presided over the US Comptrollers Association, which invested $30 trillion in pension funds. In late January Singer strategized with Governor George Pataki of New York as well as with D'Amato and Bronfman at his daughter's wedding. "Look what kind of man I am," the Rabbi mused, "doing business at my daughter's wedding."[30]

In February 1996 Hevesi and McCall wrote the Swiss banks threatening sanctions. In October Governor Pataki publicly lent his support. During the next several months local and state governments in New York, New Jersey, Rhode Island and Illinois all tabled resolutions threatening an economic boycott unless the Swiss banks came clean. In May 1997 the city of Los Angeles, withdrawing

---

[29] Bower, *Nazi Gold*, 315. Vincent, *Silent Partners*, 211. Rickman, *Swiss Banks*, 184 (Volcker).

[30] Levin, *Last Deposit*, 187–8, 125.

hundreds of millions of dollars in pension funds from a Swiss bank, imposed the first sanctions. Hevesi quickly followed suit with sanctions in New York. California, Massachusetts, and Illinois joined in within days.

"I want $3 billion or northward," Bronfman proclaimed in December 1997, "in order to end it all, the class-action suits, the Volcker process and the rest." Meanwhile, D'Amato and New York State banking officials sought to block the newly formed United Bank of Switzerland (a merger of major Swiss banks) from operating in the United States. "If the Swiss are going to keep digging their heels in, then I'll have to ask all US shareholders to suspend their dealings with the Swiss," Bronfman warned in March 1998. "It's coming to a point where it has to resolve itself or it has to be total war." In April the Swiss started buckling under the pressure, but still resisted abject surrender. (Through 1997 the Swiss reportedly spent $500 million to fend off the Holocaust industry attacks.) "There's a virulent cancer throughout the Swiss society," Melvyn Weiss, one of the class-action lawyers, lamented. "We gave them an opportunity to get rid of it with a massive dose of radiation at a cost that is very small and they've turned it down." In June the Swiss banks put forth a "final offer" of $600 million. ADL head Abraham Foxman, shocked by *Swiss* arrogance, could barely contain his rage: "This ultimatum is an insult to the memory of the victims, their survivors and to those in the Jewish community who in good faith reached to the Swiss to work together to resolve this most difficult matter."[31]

In July 1998 Hevesi and McCall threatened stiff new sanctions.

[31] Levin, *Last Deposit*, 218. Rickman, *Swiss Banks*, 214, 223, 221.

New Jersey, Pennsylvania, Connecticut, Florida, Michigan, and California joined in within days. In mid-August the Swiss finally caved in.
In a class-action settlement mediated by Judge Korman, the Swiss
agreed to pay $1.25 billion. "The aim of the additional payment," a
Swiss banks press release read, "is to avert the threat of sanctions as
well as long and costly court proceedings."[32]

"You have been a true pioneer in this saga," Israeli Prime Minister
Benjamin Netanyahu congratulated D'Amato. "The result is not only
an achievement in material terms but a moral victory and a triumph
of the spirit."[33] Pity he didn't say "the will."

The $1.25 billion settlement with Switzerland covered basically
three classes – claimants to dormant Swiss accounts, refugees denied
Swiss asylum, and victims of slave labor which Swiss benefited from.[34]
For all the righteous indignation about the "perfidious Swiss," however, the comparable American record is, on all these counts, just as
bad, if not worse. I will return presently to the matter of dormant
US accounts. Like Switzerland, the US denied entry to Jewish
refugees fleeing Nazism before and during World War II. Yet the
American government hasn't seen fit to compensate, say, Jewish

---

[32] Rickman, *Swiss Banks*, 231.

[33] Ibid. Rickman fittingly entitled this chapter of his account, "Boycotts and
Diktats."

[34] For the complete text of the "Class Action Settlement Agreement," see
Independent Committee of Eminent Persons, *Report on Dormant Accounts of
Victims of Nazi Persecution in Swiss Banks* (Bern: 1999), Appendix O. In addition
to the $200 million Special Fund and the $1.25 billion class-action settlement,
the Holocaust industry finagled another $70 million from the United States
and its allies during a 1997 London conference on the Swiss gold.

refugees aboard the ill-fated ship *St. Louis*. Imagine the reaction if the thousands of Central American and Haitian refugees who were denied asylum after fleeing US-sponsored death squads sought compensation here. And, although dwarfed in size and resources by the United States, Switzerland admitted just as many Jewish refugees as the US (approximately 20,000) during the Nazi holocaust.[35]

The only means to atone for past sins, American politicians lectured Switzerland, was providing material compensation. Stuart Eizenstat, Undersecretary for Commerce and Clinton's Special Envoy for Property Restitution, deemed Swiss compensation to Jewry "an important litmus test of this generation's willingness to face the past and to rectify the wrongs of the past." Although they couldn't be "held responsible for what took place years ago," D'Amato acknowledged during the same Senate hearing, the Swiss still had "a duty of accountability and of attempting to do what is right at this point in time." Publicly endorsing the WJC's compensation demands, President Clinton likewise reflected that "we must confront and, as best

---

[35] For US policy on Jewish refugees during these years, see David S. Wyman, *Paper Walls* (New York: 1985), and *The Abandonment of the Jews* (New York: 1984). For Swiss policy, see Independent Commission of Experts, Switzerland – Second World War, *Switzerland and Refugees in the Nazi Era* (Bern: 1999). A similar mix of factors – economic downturn, xenophobia, anti-Semitism, and, later, security – accounted for the restrictive American and Swiss quotas. Recalling the "hypocrisy in the speeches by other nations, especially the United States which was completely uninterested in liberalizing its immigration laws," the Independent Commission, although harshly critical of Switzerland, reports that its refugee policy was "like the governments of most other states." (42, 263) I found no mention of this point in the extensive US media coverage of the Commission's critical findings.

we can, right the terrible injustice of the past." "History does not have a statute of limitations," chairman James Leach said during the House Banking Committee hearings, and "the past must never be forgotten." "It should be made clear," bipartisan Congressional leaders wrote in a letter to the Secretary of State, that the "response on this restitution matter will be seen as a test of respect for basic human rights and the rule of law." And in an address to the Swiss Parliament, Secretary of State Madeleine Albright explained that the economic benefits accruing to the Swiss from withheld Jewish accounts "were passed along to subsequent generations and that is why the world now looks to the people of Switzerland, not to assume responsibility for actions taken by their forebears, but to be generous in doing what can be done at this point to right past wrongs."[36] Noble sentiments all, but nowhere to be heard – unless they are being actively ridiculed – when it comes to African-American compensation for slavery.[37]

[36] Hearings before the Committee on Banking, Housing, and Urban Affairs, United States Senate, 15 May 1997 (Eizenstat and D'Amato). Hearings before the Committee on Banking, Housing, and Urban Affairs, United States Senate, 23 April 1996 (Bronfman, quoting Clinton and letter of Congressional leaders). Hearings before the Committee on Banking and Financial Services, House of Representatives, 11 December 1996 (Leach). Hearings before the Committee on Banking and Financial Services, House of Representatives, 25 June 1997 (Leach). Rickman, *Swiss Banks*, 204 (Albright).

[37] The only discordant note during the multiple Congressional hearings on Holocaust compensation was sounded by Congresswoman Maxine Waters of California. While registering "1000 percent" support "to get justice for all of the victims of the Holocaust," Waters also questioned "how to take this format and use it to deal with slave labor of my ancestors here in the United States. It's very strange to sit here . . . without wondering what I could be doing . . . to acknowledge slave labor in the United States. . . . Reparations

It remains unclear how "needy Holocaust survivors" will fare in the final settlement. Gizella Weisshaus, the first claimant of a dormant Swiss account to sue, has discharged her attorney, Edward Fagan, bitterly charging that he used her. Still, Fagan's bill to the court totaled $4 million in fees. Total attorney fee demands run to $15 million, with "many" billing at a rate of $600 per hour. One lawyer is asking $2,400 for reading Tom Bower's book, *Nazi Gold*. "Jewish groups and survivors," New York's *Jewish Week* reported, "are taking off the gloves as they vie for a share of the Swiss banks' $1.25 billion Holocaust-era settlement." Plaintiffs and survivors maintain that all the money should go directly to them. Jewish organizations, however, are demanding a piece of the action. Denouncing the aggrandizement

---

in the African-American community have been basically condemned as a radical idea, and many of those . . . who tried so hard to get this issue before the Congress have literally been ridiculed." Specifically she proposed that government agencies directed to achieving Holocaust compensation be directed as well to achieving compensation for "domestic slave labor." "The gentle lady raises an extraordinarily profound subject," James Leach of the House Banking Committee replied, "and the Chair will take it under advisement. . . . The profoundness of the issue you raise in an American historical setting as well as in the human rights setting is deep." The issue will undoubtedly be deposited deep in the Committee's memory hole. (Hearings before the Committee on Banking and Financial Services, House of Representatives, 9 February 2000) Randall Robinson, who is currently leading a campaign to compensate African-Americans for slavery, juxtaposed the US government's "silence" on this theft "even as the US Undersecretary of State, Stuart Eizenstat, labored to make 16 German companies compensate Jews used as slave laborers during the Nazi era." (Randall Robinson, "Compensate the Forgotten Victims of America's Slavery Holocaust," in *Los Angeles Times* [11 February 2000]; cf. Randall Robinson, *The Debt* [New York: 2000], 245) of the Jewish organizations, Greta Beer, a key Congressional witness against the Swiss banks, beseeched Judge Korman's court that "I don't want to be crushed underfoot like a little insect." Its solicitude for "needy Holocaust survivors" notwithstanding, the WJC wants nearly half the Swiss monies earmarked for Jewish organizations and "Holocaust education." The Simon Wiesenthal Center maintains that if "worthy" Jewish organizations receive monies, "a portion should go to Jewish educational centers." As they "angle" for a bigger share of the loot, Reform and Orthodox organizations each claim that the 6 million dead would have preferred their branch of Judaism as financial beneficiary. Meanwhile, the Holocaust industry forced Switzerland into a settlement because time was allegedly of the essence: "needy Holocaust survivors are dying every day." Once the Swiss signed away the money, however, the urgency miraculously passed. More than a year after the settlement was reached there was still no distribution plan. By the time the money is finally divvied out all the "needy Holocaust survivors" will probably be dead. In fact, as of December 1999, less than half of the $200 million "Special Fund for Needy Victims of the Holocaust" established in February 1997 had been distributed to actual victims. After lawyers' fees have been paid, the Swiss monies will then flow into the coffers of "worthy" Jewish organizations.[38]

---

[38] Philip Lentz, "Reparation Woes," in *Crain's* (15–21 November 1999). Michael Shapiro, "Lawyers in Swiss Bank Settlement Submit Bill, Outraging Jewish Groups," in *Jewish Telegraphic Agency* (23 November 1999). Rebecca Spence, "Hearings on Legal Fees in Swiss Bank Case," in *Forward* (26 November 1999). James Bone, "Holocaust Survivors Protest Over Legal Fee," in *The Times* (London) (1 December 1999). Devlin Barrett, "Holocaust Assets," in *New*

"No settlement can possibly be defended," Burt Neuborne, a New York University law professor and member of the class-action legal team, wrote in the *New York Times*, "if it allows the Holocaust to stand as a profit-making enterprise for the Swiss banks." Edgar Bronfman movingly testified before the House Banking Committee that the Swiss should not "be allowed to make a profit from the ashes of the Holocaust." On the other hand, Bronfman recently acknowledged that the WJC treasury has amassed no less than "roughly $7 billion" in compensation monies.[39]

The authoritative reports on the Swiss banks have meanwhile been published. One can now judge whether in fact there was, as Bower claims, a "fifty-year Swiss-Nazi conspiracy to steal billions from Europe's Jews and Holocaust survivors."

In July 1998 the Independent (Bergier) Commission of Experts issued its report, *Switzerland and Gold Transactions in the Second World War*.[40] The Commission confirmed that Swiss banks purchased gold

---

York Post (2 December 1999). Stewart Ain, "Religious Strife Erupts In Swiss Money Fight," in *Jewish Week* (14 January 2000) ("angle"). Adam Dickter, "Discord in the Court," in *Jewish Week* (21 January 2000). Swiss Fund for Needy Victims of the Holocaust/Shoa, "Overview on Finances, Payments and Pending Applications" (30 November 1999). Holocaust survivors in Israel never received any of the Special Fund monies earmarked for them; see Yair Sheleg, "Surviving Israeli Bureaucracy," in *Haaretz* (6 February 2000).

[39] Burt Neuborne, "Totaling the Sum of Swiss Guilt," in *New York Times* (24 June 1998). Hearings before the Committee on Banking and Financial Services, House of Representatives, 11 December 1996. "Holocaust-Konferenz in Stockholm," in *Frankfurter Allgemeine Zeitung* (26 January 2000) (Bronfman).

[40] Independent Commission of Experts, Switzerland – Second World War, *Switzerland and Gold Transactions in the Second World War, Interim Report* (Bern: 1998).

from Nazi Germany, worth about $4 billion in current values, knowing that it had been plundered from the central banks of occupied Europe. Throughout the hearings on Capitol Hill, members of Congress expressed shock that Swiss banks had trafficked in looted assets and, even worse, still indulged these egregious practices. Deploring the fact that corrupt politicians deposit their ill-gotten gains in Swiss banks, one Congressman called on Switzerland to finally enact legislation against "this secret movement of money by . . . people of political prominence or leadership, of people looting their treasury." Bewailing the "number of international, high profile corrupt government officials and businesspeople who have found sanctuary for their substantial wealth in Swiss banks," another Congressman wondered aloud whether "the Swiss banking system is accommodating this generation's thugs, and the countries they represent, in . . . ways that sanctuary was given to the Nazi regime 55 years ago?"[41] Truly the problem warrants concern. Annually an estimated $100–$200 billion arising from political corruption is sent across borders worldwide and deposited in private banks. The Congressional banking committee reprimands would have carried more weight, however, if fully half

---

[41] Hearings before the Committee on Banking and Financial Services, House of Representatives, 11 December 1996. Called as an expert witness, University of North Carolina historian Gerhard L. Weinberg sanctimoniously testified that the "position of the Swiss Government at the time and in the immediate postwar years was always that looting is legal," and that "priority number one" of the Swiss banks was "making as much money as possible . . . and to do so regardless of the legalities, morality and decency or anything else." (Hearings before the Committee on Banking and Financial Services, House of Representatives, 25 June 1997)

this "illegal flight capital" weren't deposited in American banks with the complete sanction of US law.[42] Recent beneficiaries of this legal US "sanctuary" include Raul Salinas de Gortari, the brother of Mexico's former president, and the family of former Nigerian dictator General Sani Abacha. "The gold looted by Adolf Hitler and his henchmen," Jean Ziegler, a Swiss parliamentarian fiercely critical of the Swiss banks, observes, "does not differ in essence from the blood money" now held in the private Swiss accounts of Third World dictators. "Millions of men, women, and children were driven to their deaths by Hitler's licensed thieves," and "hundreds of thousands of children die annually of disease and malnutrition" in the Third World because "tyrants despoiled their countries with the aid of Swiss financial sharks."[43] And with the aid of American financial sharks as well. I leave to one side the even more important point that many of these tyrants were installed and maintained by US power and authorized by the United States to despoil their countries.

On the specific question of the Nazi holocaust, the Independent Commission concluded that the Swiss banks did purchase "bars containing gold looted by Nazi criminals from the victims of work camps and extermination camps." They didn't, however, knowingly do so: "there is no indication that the decision-makers at the Swiss central bank knew that bars containing such gold were being shipped to Switzerland by the Reichsbank." The Commission put the value of

---

[42] Raymond W. Baker, "The Biggest Loophole in the Free-Market System," in *Washington Quarterly* (Autumn 1999). Although not sanctioned by US law, much of the $500 billion–$1 trillion annually "laundered" from the drug trade is also "safely deposited into US banks." (ibid.)

[43] Ziegler, *The Swiss*, xii; cf. 19, 265.

THE DOUBLE SHAKEDOWN 111

"victim gold" unwittingly purchased by Switzerland at $134,428, or about $1 million in current values. This figure includes "victim gold" stripped from Jewish as well as non-Jewish camp inmates.[44]

In December 1999 the Independent (Volcker) Committee of Eminent Persons issued its *Report on Dormant Accounts of Victims of Nazi Persecution in Swiss Banks*.[45] The *Report* documents the findings of an exhaustive audit that lasted three years and cost no less than $500 million.[46] Its central finding on the "treatment of dormant accounts of victims of Nazi persecution" merits extended quotation:

[F]or victims of Nazi persecution there was no evidence of systematic discrimination, obstruction of access, misappropriation, or violation of document retention requirements of Swiss law. However, the Report also criticizes the actions of some banks in their treatment of the accounts of victims of Nazi persecution. The word "some" in the preceding sentence needs to be emphasized since the criticized actions refer mainly to those of specific banks in their handling of individual accounts of victims of Nazi persecution in the context of an investigation of 254 banks covering a period of about 60 years. For the criticized actions, the Report also recognizes that there were mitigating circumstances for the conduct of the banks involved in these activities. The Report acknowledges, moreover, that there is ample evidence of

[44] *Switzerland and Gold Transactions in the Second World War*, IV, 48.

[45] Independent Committee of Eminent Persons, *Report on Dormant Accounts of Victims of Nazi Persecution in Swiss Banks* (Bern: 1999). (hereafter *Report*)

[46] The "external cost" of the audit was put at $200 million. (*Report*, p. 4, paragraph 17) The cost to the Swiss banks was put at another $300 million. (Swiss Federal Banking Commission, press release, 6 December 1999)

many cases in which banks actively sought out missing account holders or their heirs, including Holocaust victims, and paid account balances of dormant accounts to the proper parties.

The paragraph mildly concludes that "the Committee believes the criticized actions are of sufficient importance that it is desirable to document in this section the things that did go wrong so that it is possible to learn from the past rather than repeat its mistakes."[47]

The *Report* also found that, although the Committee couldn't track down all the bank records for the "Relevant Period" (1933–45), destruction of records without detection "would be difficult, if not impossible," and that "in fact, no evidence of systematic destruction of account records for the purpose of concealing past behavior has been found." It concludes that the percentage of records recovered (60 percent) was "truly extraordinary" and "truly remarkable," especially given that Swiss law does not require retention of records beyond 10 years.[48]

Yet, compare the *New York Times*'s rendering of the Volcker Committee findings. Under an editorial headline, "The Deceptions of Swiss Banks,"[49] the *Times* reported that the Committee found "no conclusive evidence" that Swiss banks mishandled dormant Jewish

[47] *Report*, Annex 5, p. 81, paragraph 1 (cf. Part I, pp. 13–15, paragraphs 41–9).

[48] *Report:* Part I, p. 6, paragraph 22 ("no evidence"); Part I, p. 6, paragraph 23 (banking laws and percentage); Annex 4, p. 58, paragraph 5 ("truly extraordinary") and Annex 5, p. 81, paragraph 3 ("truly remarkable") (cf. Part I, p. 15, paragraph 47, Part I, p. 17, paragraph 58, Annex 7, p. 107, paragraphs 3, 9)

[49] "The Deceptions of Swiss Banks," in *New York Times* (7 December 1999).

accounts. Yet the *Report* categorically stated "no evidence." The *Times* goes on to state that the Committee "found that Swiss banks had somehow managed to lose track of a shockingly large number of these accounts." Yet the *Report* found that the Swiss preserved records of a "truly extraordinary," "truly remarkable" number. Finally, the *Times* reports that, according to the Committee, "many banks had cruelly and deceptively turned away family members trying to recover lost assets." In fact, the *Report* emphasizes that only "some" banks misbehaved and that there were "mitigating circumstances" in these cases, and it points out as well the "many cases" in which banks actively sought out legitimate claimants.

The *Report* does fault the Swiss banks for not being "straightforward and forthright" in prior audits of dormant Holocaust-era accounts. Nonetheless, it seems to credit the shortfall in these audits more to technical factors than malfeasance.[50] The *Report* identifies 54,000 accounts with a "probable or possible relationship with victims of Nazi persecution." But it judges that only in the case of half this number – 25,000 – was the likelihood significant enough to warrant publication of account names. The estimated current value of 10,000 of these accounts for which some information was available runs to $170–$260

---

[50] *Report*, Annex 5, p. 81, paragraph 2. *Report*, Annex 5, pp. 87–8, paragraph 27: "There are a variety of explanations for the substantial under-reporting in the early surveys, but some of the main causes can be attributed to the Swiss banks' use of narrow definitions of 'dormant' accounts; their exclusion of certain types of accounts from their searches or inadequate research; their failure to investigate accounts under certain minimum balances; or their failure to consider account holders to be victims of Nazi violence or persecution unless relatives made such claims at the bank."

million. It proved impossible to estimate the current value of the remaining accounts.[51] The total value of actual dormant Holocaust-era accounts will likely climb much higher than the $32 million originally estimated by the Swiss banks, but will still fall staggeringly short of the $7–$20 billion claimed by the WJC. In subsequent Congressional testimony, Volcker observed that the number of Swiss accounts "probably or possibly" related to Holocaust victims was "many times as large as that emerging from previous Swiss investigations." However, he continued: "I emphasize the words 'probably or possibly' because, except in a relatively few cases, after more than half a century, we were not able to identify with certainty an irrefutable relationship between victims and account holders."[52]

The most explosive finding of the Volcker Committee went unreported in the American media. Alongside Switzerland, the Com-

---

[51] *Report*, p. 10, paragraph 30 ("possible or probable"); p. 20, paragraphs 73–5 (significant probability for 25,000 accounts). *Report*, Annex 4, pp. 65–7, paragraphs 20–6, and p. 72, paragraphs 40–3 (current values). In accordance with the *Report* recommendation, the Swiss Federal Banking Commission agreed in March 2000 to publish the 25,000 account names. ("Swiss Federal Banking Commission Follows Volcker Recommendations," press release, 30 March 2000)

[52] Hearings before the Committee on Banking and Financial Services, House of Representatives, 9 February 2000 (quoted from Volcker's prepared testimony). Compare the caveats entered by the Swiss Federal Banking Commission that "all indications on possible current values of accounts identified are essentially based on assumptions and projections," and that "only in the case of about 1,200 accounts . . . has actual evidence be [sic] found, supported by contemporary in-house banking sources, that the account owners were actually victims of the Holocaust." (press release, 6 December 1999)

mittee observes, the US was *also* a primary safe haven for transferable Jewish assets in Europe:

> The anticipation of war and economic distress, as well as the persecution of Jews and other minorities by the Nazis prior to and during World War II, caused many people, including the victims of this persecution, to move their assets to countries deemed to provide safe havens (importantly including the United States and the United Kingdom). . . . In view of neutral Switzerland's borders with Axis and Axis-occupied countries, Swiss banks and other Swiss financial intermediaries were also recipients of a portion of the assets in search of safety.

An important appendix lists the "favored destinations" of Jewish transferable assets in Europe. The main stated destinations were the US and Switzerland. (Great Britain came in a "low third" as a stated destination.)[53]

The obvious question is, What happened to the dormant Holocaust-era accounts in *American* banks? The House Banking Committee did call one expert witness to testify on this issue. Seymour Rubin, currently a professor at American University, served as deputy chief of the US delegation in the Swiss negotiations after World War II. Under the auspices of American Jewish organizations Rubin also worked during the 1950s with a "group of experts on Jewish communal life in Europe" to identify dormant Holocaust-era accounts

---

[53] *Report*, p. 2, paragraph 8 (cf. p. 23, paragraph 92). *Report*, Appendix S, p. A-134; for a more precise breakdown, cf. pp. A-135ff.

in US banks. In his House testimony Rubin stated that, after a most superficial and rudimentary audit of just New York banks, the value of these accounts was put at $6 million. Jewish organizations requested this sum for "needy survivors" from Congress (abandoned dormant accounts in the US are transferred to the state under the doctrine of escheat). Rubin then recalled:

> [T]he initial estimate of $6 million was rejected by potential Congressional sponsors of the necessary legislation and a limit of $3 million was used in the original draft legislation. . . . In the event, the $3 million figure was slashed in Committee hearings to $1 million. Legislative action further reduced the amount to $500,000. Even that amount was opposed by the Bureau of the Budget, which proposed a limit of $250,000. The legislation however passed with the $500,000.

"The United States," Rubin concluded, "took only very limited measures to identify heirless assets in the United States, and made available . . . a mere $500,000, in contrast to the $32,000,000 acknowledged by Swiss banks even prior to the Volcker inquiry."[54] In other words, *the US record is much worse than the Swiss record*. It bears emphasis that, apart from a fleeting remark by Eizenstat, there was no other mention of the dormant US accounts during the House and Senate banking committee hearings devoted to the Swiss

[54] Hearings before the Committee on Banking and Financial Services, House of Representatives, 25 June 1997 (quoted from Rubin's prepared testimony). (For background, see Seymour J. Rubin and Abba P. Schwartz, "Refugees and Reparations," in *Law and Contemporary Problems* [Duke University School of Law: 1951], 286–9.)

banks. Moreover, although Rubin plays a pivotal role in the many secondary accounts of the Swiss banks affair — Bower devotes scores of pages to this "crusader in the State Department" — none mention his House testimony. During the House hearing Rubin also expressed "a certain amount of skepticism with respect to the large amounts [in dormant Swiss accounts] which are being talked about." Needless to say, Rubin's precise insights on this matter were also studiously ignored.

Where was the Congressional hue and cry over "perfidious" American bankers? One member after another of the Senate and House banking committees clamored for the Swiss to "finally pay up." None, however, called on the US to do so. Rather, a House Banking Committee member shamelessly averred — with Bronfman agreeing — that "only" Switzerland "has failed to show the courage to confront its own history."[55] Unsurprisingly, the Holocaust industry didn't launch a campaign to investigate US banks. An audit of our banks on the scale of the Swiss audit would cost American taxpayers not millions but billions of dollars.[56] By the time it was completed American Jews would be seeking asylum in Munich. Courage has its limits.

Already in the late 1940s, when the US was pressing Switzerland to identify dormant Jewish accounts, the Swiss protested that

---

[55] Hearings before the Committee on Banking and Financial Services, House of Representatives, 25 June 1997.

[56] Switzerland's population stood at 4 million for the "Relevant Period" of 1933–45 as compared to the US population of over 130 million. Every Swiss bank account opened, closed or dormant during these years was audited by the Volcker committee.

Americans should first attend to their own backyard.[57] In mid-1997 New York Governor Pataki announced the creation of a State Commission on the Recovery Of Holocaust Victims' Assets to process claims against Swiss banks. Unimpressed, the Swiss suggested that the commission might more usefully process claims against US and Israeli banks.[58] Indeed Bower recalls that Israeli bankers had "refused to release lists of dormant accounts of Jews" after the 1948 war, and recently it has been reported that "unlike countries in Europe, Israel's banks and Zionist organizations are resisting pressure to set up independent commissions to establish how much property and how many dormant accounts were held by Holocaust survivors, and how the owners can be located" (*Financial Times*). (European Jews purchased plots of land and opened bank accounts in Palestine during the British Mandate to support the Zionist enterprise or prepare for future immigration.) In October 1998, the WJC and WJRO "reached a decision in principle to refrain from dealing with the subject of assets in Israel of Holocaust victims on the ground that responsibility for this lay with the Israeli government" (*Haaretz*). The writ of these Jewish organizations thus runs to Switzerland but not to the Jewish state. The most sensational charge leveled against the Swiss banks was that they required death certificates from the heirs of Nazi holocaust victims. Israeli banks have also demanded such documentation. One searches in vain, however, for denunciations of the "perfidious Israelis." To demonstrate that "no moral equivalence can be drawn

---

[57] Levin, *Last Deposit*, 23. Bower, *Nazi Gold*, 256. Bower deems this Swiss demand "unanswerable rhetoric." Unanswerable no doubt, but why rhetoric?

[58] Rickman, *Swiss Banks*, 194–5.

between banks in Israel and Switzerland," the *New York Times* quoted a former Israeli legislator: "Here it was negligence at best; in Switzerland it was a crime."[59] Comment is superfluous.

In May 1998 a Presidential Advisory Commission on Holocaust Assets in the United States was charged by Congress with "conducting original research on the fate of assets taken from victims of the Holocaust that came into the possession of the U.S. Federal government" and "advising the President on policies that should be adopted to make restitution to the rightful owners of stolen property or their heirs." "The Commission's work demonstrates irrefutably," Commission chair Bronfman declared, "that we in the United States are willing to hold ourselves to the same high standard of truth about Holocaust assets to which we have held other nations." Yet a presidential advisory commission with a total budget of $6 million is rather different from a comprehensive $500 million external audit of a nation's entire banking system with unfettered access to all bank records.[60] To dispel any lingering doubts that the US stood in the forefront of efforts to restore Holocaust-era stolen Jewish assets, James Leach, chairman of the House Banking Committee, proudly

---

[59] Bower, *Nazi Gold*, 350–1. Akiva Eldar, "UK: Israel Didn't Hand Over Compensation to Survivors," in *Haaretz* (21 February 2000). Judy Dempsey, "Jews Find It Hard to Reclaim Wartime Property In Israel," in *Financial Times* (1 April 2000). Jack Katzenell, "Israel Has WWII Assets," in *Associated Press* (13 April 2000). Joel Greenberg, "Hunt for Holocaust Victims' Property Turns in New Direction: Toward Israel," in *New York Times* (15 April 2000). Akiva Eldar, "People and Politics," in *Haaretz* (27 April 2000).

[60] For information on the Commission, see *www.pcha.gov* (Bronfman quoted from a 21 November 1999 Commission press release).

announced in February 2000 that a North Carolina museum had returned one painting to an Austrian family. "It underscores United States accountability . . . and I think that is something that this Committee ought to stress."[61]

For the Holocaust industry, the Swiss banks affair – like the postwar torments endured by Swiss Holocaust "survivor" Binjamin Wilkomirski – was yet further proof of an ineradicable and irrational Gentile malice. The affair pointed up the gross insensitivity of even a "liberal democratic, European country," Itamar Levin concludes, to "those who carried the physical and emotional scars of the worst crime in history." An April 1997 Tel Aviv University study reported "an unmistakable rise" in Swiss anti-Semitism. Yet this ominous development couldn't possibly be connected with the Holocaust industry's shakedown of Switzerland. "Jews do not make anti-Semitism," Bronfman sniffed. "Anti-Semites make anti-Semitism."[62]

Material compensation for the Holocaust "is the greatest moral test facing Europe at the end of the twentieth century," Itamar Levin maintains. "This will be the real test of the Continent's treatment of the Jewish people."[63] Indeed, emboldened by its success in shaking down the Swiss, the Holocaust industry moved quickly to "test" the rest of Europe. The next stop was Germany.

After the Holocaust industry settled with Switzerland in August 1998, it deployed the same winning strategy against Germany in

---

[61] Hearings before the Committee on Banking and Financial Services, House of Representatives, 9 February 2000.

[62] Levin, *Last Deposit*, 223, 204. "Swiss Defensive About WWII Role," in *Associated Press* (15 March 2000). *Time* (24 February 1997) (Bronfman).

[63] Levin, *Last Deposit*, 224.

September. The same three legal teams (Hausfeld–Weiss, Fagan–Swift, and the World Council of Orthodox Jewish Communities) initiated class-action lawsuits against German private industry, demanding no less than $20 billion in compensation. Brandishing the threat of an economic boycott, New York City Comptroller Hevesi began to "monitor" the negotiations in April 1999. The House Banking Committee held hearings in September. Congresswoman Carolyn Maloney declared that "the passage of time must not be an excuse for unjust enrichment" (at any rate, from Jewish slave labor – African-American slave labor is another story) while Committee chairman Leach, reading from the same old script, intoned that "history has no statute of limitations." German companies doing business in the United States, Stuart Eizenstat told the Committee, "value their good will here, and will want to continue the kind of good citizenship in the US and Germany that they've always displayed." Forgoing diplomatic niceties, Congressman Rick Lazio bluntly urged the Committee "to focus on the private sector German companies, in particular, those who do business in the US."[64] To whip up public hysteria against Germany, the Holocaust industry took out multiple full-page newspaper advertisements in October. The awful truth did not suffice; all the Holocaust hot buttons were pressed. An ad denouncing the German pharmaceutical corporation Bayer dragged in Josef Mengele, although the evidence that Bayer "directed" his murderous experiments was nil. Recognizing that the Holocaust juggernaut was irresistible, the Germans caved in to a substantial monetary settlement by year's end.

[64] Hearings before the Committee on Banking and Financial Services, House of Representatives, 14 September 1999.

The Times of London credited this capitulation to the "Holocash" campaign in the United States. "We could not have reached agreement," Eizenstat later told the House Banking Committee, "without the personal involvement and leadership of President Clinton . . . as well as other senior officials" in the US government.[65]

The Holocaust industry charged that Germany had a "moral and legal obligation" to compensate former Jewish slave laborers. "These slave laborers deserve a small measure of justice," Eizenstat pleaded, "in the few years remaining in their lives." Yet, as indicated above, it is simply untrue that they hadn't received any compensation. Jewish slave laborers were covered under the original agreements with Germany compensating concentration camp inmates. The German government indemnified former Jewish slave laborers for "deprivation of liberty" and for "harm to life and limb." Only wages withheld were not formally compensated. Those who sustained enduring injuries

---

[65] Yair Sheleg, "Not Even Minimum Wage," in *Haaretz* (6 October 1999). William Drozdiak, "Germans Up Offer to Nazis' Slave Laborers," in *Washington Post* (18 November 1999). Burt Herman, "Nazi Labor Talks End Without Pact," in *Forward* (20 November 1999). "Bayer's Biggest Headache," in *New York Times* (5 October 1999). Jan Cienski, "Wartime Slave-Labour Survivors' Ads Hit Back," in *National Post* (7 October 1999). Edmund L. Andrews, "Germans To Set Up $5.1 Billion Fund For Nazis' Slaves," in *New York Times* (15 December 1999). Edmund L. Andrews, "Germany Accepts $5.1 billion Accord to End Claims of Nazi Slave Workers," in *New York Times* (18 December 1999). Allan Hall, "Slave Labour List Names 255 German Companies," in *The Times* (London) (9 December 1999). Hearings before the Committee on Banking and Financial Services, House of Representatives, 9 February 2000 (quoted from Eizenstat's prepared testimony).

each received a substantial lifetime pension.[66] Germany also endowed the Jewish Claims Conference with approximately a billion dollars in current values for those Jewish ex-camp inmates who received minimum compensation. As indicated earlier, the Claims Conference, violating the agreement with Germany, used the monies instead for various pet projects. It justified this (mis)use of German compensation on the grounds that "even before the funds from Germany had become available . . . the needs of the 'needy' victims of Nazism had already been largely met."[67] Still, fifty years later the Holocaust industry was demanding money for "needy Holocaust victims" who had been living in poverty because the Germans allegedly never compensated them.

What constitutes "fair" compensation for former Jewish slave laborers is plainly an unanswerable question. One can, however, say this: According to the terms of the new settlement, Jewish former slave laborers are each supposed to receive about $7,500. If the Claims Conference had properly distributed the original German monies, many more former Jewish slave laborers would have received much more much sooner.

Whether "needy Holocaust victims" will ever see any of the new German monies is an open question. The Claims Conference wants a

---

[66] Sagi, *German Reparations*, 161. Probably a quarter of the Jewish slave laborers received such a pension, my late father (an Auschwitz inmate) among them. In fact, the Claims Conference's figure in the current negotiations for Jewish slave laborers still alive is based on those already receiving pensions and compensation from Germany! (German Parliament, 92nd session, 15 March 2000)

[67] Zweig, *German Reparations and the Jewish World*, 98; cf. 25.

large chunk set aside as its own "Special Fund." According to the *Jerusalem Report*, the Conference has "plenty to gain by ensuring that the survivors get nothing." Israeli Knesset member Michael Kleiner (Herut) lambasted the Conference as a "Judenrat, carrying on the Nazis' work in different ways." It's a "dishonest body, conducting itself with professional secrecy, and tainted by ugly public and moral corruption," he charged, "a body of darkness that is maltreating Jewish Holocaust survivors and their heirs, while it sits on a huge pile of money belonging to private individuals, but is doing everything to inherit [the money] while they are still alive."[68] Meanwhile, Stuart Eizenstat, testifying before the House Banking Committee, continued to heap praise on the "transparent process that the Jewish Material Claims Conference has had over the last 40-some-odd years." For sheer cynicism, however, Rabbi Israel Singer ranked without peer. In addition to his secretary-general post at the World Jewish Congress, Singer has served as vice-president of the Claims Conference and was chief negotiator in the German slave-labor talks. He piously reiterated to the House Banking Committee after the Swiss and German settlements that "it would be a shame" if the Holocaust compensation monies were "paid to heirs rather than survivors." "We don't want

---

[68] Conference on Jewish Material Claims Against Germany, "Position Paper — Slave Labor. Proposed Remembrance and Responsibility Fund" (15 June 1999). Netty C. Gross, "$5.1-Billion Slave Labor Deal Could Yield Little Cash For Jewish Claimants," in *Jerusalem Report* (31 January 2000). Zvi Lavi, "Kleiner (Herut): Germany Claims Conference Has Become Judenrat, Carrying on Nazi Ways," in *Globes* (24 February 2000). Yair Sheleg, "MK Kleiner: The Claims Conference Does Not Transfer Indemnifications to Shoah Survivors," in *Haaretz* (24 February 2000).

that money paid to heirs. We want that money to be paid to victims."
Yet, *Haaretz* reports that Singer has been the main proponent of using
Holocaust compensation monies "to meet the needs of the entire
Jewish people, and not just those Jews who were fortunate enough to
survive the Holocaust and live into old age."[69]

In a US Holocaust Memorial Museum publication, Henry Friedlander, the respected Nazi holocaust historian and ex-Auschwitz inmate,
sketched this numerical picture at war's end:

> If there were about 715,000 prisoners in the camps at the start of
> 1945, and at least one third – that is, about 238,000 – perished
> during spring 1945, we can assume that at most 475,000 prisoners
> survived. As Jews had been systematically murdered, and only those
> chosen for labor – in Auschwitz about 15 percent – had even a chance
> to survive, we must assume that Jews made up no more than 20
> percent of the concentration camp population.

"We can thus estimate," he concluded, "that the number of Jewish
survivors numbered no more than 100,000." Friedlander's figure for
surviving Jewish slave laborers at war's end, incidentally, is at the
high end among scholars. In an authoritative study, Leonard Dinnerstein reported: "Sixty thousand Jews . . . walked out of the concentration camps. Within a week more than 20,000 of them had died."[70]

---

[69] Hearings before the Committee on Banking and Financial Services, House of
Representatives, 9 February 2000. Yair Sheleg, "Staking a Claim to Jewish
Claims," in *Haaretz* (31 March 2000).

[70] Henry Friedlander, "Darkness and Dawn in 1945: The Nazis, the Allies, and
the Survivors," in *US Holocaust Memorial Museum, 1945 – The Year of Liberation*

In a May 1999 State Department briefing, Stuart Eizenstat, citing the figure of "groups representing them," put the total number of slave laborers, Jewish and non-Jewish, still alive at "perhaps 70–90,000."[71] Eizenstat was Chief US Envoy in the German slave-labor negotiations and worked closely with the Claims Conference.[72] This would put the total number of still living Jewish slave laborers at 14,000–18,000 (20 percent of 70–90,000). Yet, as it entered into negotiations with Germany, the Holocaust industry demanded compensation for 135,000 still living former Jewish slave laborers. The total number of still living former slave laborers, Jewish and non-Jewish, was put at 250,000.[73] In other words, the number of former Jewish slave laborers still alive increased nearly tenfold from May 1999, and the ratio between living Jewish and non-Jewish slave laborers drastically shifted. In fact, to believe the Holocaust industry, more former Jewish slave laborers are alive today than a

---

(Washington: 1995), 11–35. Dinnerstein, *America and the Survivors of the Holocaust*, 28. Israeli historian Shlomo Shafir reports "the estimate of Jewish survivors at the end of the war in Europe vary from 50,000 to 70,000" (*Ambiguous Relations*, 384n1). Friedlander's total figure for surviving slave laborers, Jewish and non-Jewish, is standard; see Benjamin Ferencz, *Less Than Slaves* (Cambridge: 1979) – "approximately half a million persons were found more or less alive in the camps that were liberated by the Allied armies" (xvii; cf. 240n5).

71 Stuart Eizenstat, Undersecretary of State for Economic, Business and Agricultural Affairs, Chief US Envoy in German Slave-Labor Negotiations, State Department Briefing, 12 May 1999.

72 See Eizenstat's "remarks" at the Conference on Jewish Material Claims Against Germany and Austria Annual Meeting (New York: 14 July 1999).

73 Toby Axelrod, "$5.2 Billion Slave-Labor Deal Only the Start," in *Jewish Bulletin* (12 December 1999; citing *Jewish Telegraphic Agency*).

half-century ago. "What a tangled web we weave," Sir Walter Scott wrote, "when first we practice to deceive."

As the Holocaust industry plays with numbers to boost its compensation claims, anti-Semites gleefully mock the "Jew liars" who even "huckster" their dead. In juggling these numbers the Holocaust industry, however unintentionally, whitewashes Nazism. Raul Hilberg, the leading authority on the Nazi holocaust, puts the figure for Jews murdered at 5.1 million.[74] Yet, if 135,000 former Jewish slave laborers are still alive today, some 600,000 must have survived the war. That's at least a half-million more than standard estimates. One would then have to deduct this half-million from the 5.1 million figure of those killed. Not only does the "6 Million" figure become more untenable but the numbers of the Holocaust industry are rapidly approaching those of Holocaust deniers. Consider that Nazi leader Heinrich Himmler put the total camp population in January 1945 at a little over 700,000 and that, according to Friedlander, about one-third this number was killed off by May. Yet if Jews constituted only 20 percent of the surviving camp population and, as the Holocaust industry implies, 600,000 Jewish inmates survived the war, then fully 3 million inmates in total must have survived. By the Holocaust industry's reckoning, concentration camp conditions couldn't have been harsh at all; in fact, one must suppose a remarkably high fertility and remarkably low mortality rate.[75]

[74] Hilberg, *The Destruction* (1985), v. iii, Appendix B.

[75] In an interview with *Die Berliner Zeitung*, I cast doubt on the Claims Conference's 135,000 figure, citing Friedlander. The Claims Conference curtly stated in its rebuttal that the 135,000 figure was "based on the best and most trustworthy sources and is therefore correct." Not one of these alleged

The standard claim is that the Final Solution was a uniquely efficient, assembly-line, industrial extermination.[76] But if, as the Holocaust industry suggests, many hundreds of thousands of Jews survived, the Final Solution couldn't have been so efficient after all. It must have been a haphazard affair — exactly what Holocaust deniers argue. *Les extrêmes se touchent.*

In a recent interview Raul Hilberg underscored that numbers do matter in comprehending the Nazi holocaust. Indeed, the Claims Conference's revised figures radically call into question its own understanding. According to the Claims Conference's "position paper" on slave labor in its negotiations with Germany: "Slave labor was one of the three main methods used by the Nazis to murder Jews — the others being shooting and gassing. One of the purposes of slave labor was to work the individuals to death. . . . The term slave is an imprecise word in this context. In general slave masters have an interest to preserve the life and condition of their slaves. However,

---

sources, however, was identified. ("Die Ausbeutung jüdischen Leidens," in *Berliner Zeitung*, 29–30 January 2000; "Gegendarstellung der Jewish Claims Conference," in *Berliner Zeitung*, 1 February 2000) Replying to my criticisms in an interview with *Der Tagesspiegel*, the Claims Conference maintained that some 700,000 Jewish slave laborers survived the war, 350,000–400,000 on the territory of the Reich and 300,000 in concentration camps elsewhere. Pressed to supply scholarly sources, the Claims Conference indignantly refused. Suffice to say that these figures bear no resemblance to any known scholarship on the topic. (Eva Schweitzer, "Entschaedigung für Zwangsarbeiter," in *Tagesspiegel*, 6 March 2000)

[76] "Never before in history," Hilberg has observed, "had people been killed on an assembly-line basis." (*Destruction*, v. iii, 863). The classic treatment of this topic is Zygmunt Bauman's *Modernity and the Holocaust*.

the Nazi plan for the 'slaves' was that their work potential be utilized and then the 'slaves' should be exterminated." Apart from Holocaust deniers, no one has yet disputed that Nazism consigned slave laborers to this horrific fate. How can one reconcile these established facts, however, with the claim that many hundreds of thousands of Jewish slave laborers survived the camps? Hasn't the Claims Conference breached the wall separating the ghastly truth about the Nazi holocaust from Holocaust denial?[77]

In a full-page *New York Times* advertisement, Holocaust industry luminaries such as Elie Wiesel, Rabbi Marvin Hier, and Steven T. Katz condemned "Syria's Denial of the Holocaust." The text decried an editorial in an official Syrian government newspaper that claimed Israel "invents stories about the Holocaust" in order to "receive more money from Germany and other Western establishments." Regrettably, the Syrian charge is true. Yet the irony, lost on both the Syrian government and the signatories to the ad, is that these stories themselves of many hundreds of thousands of survivors constitute a form of Holocaust denial.[78]

---

[77] Guttenplan, "Holocaust on Trial." (Hilberg) Conference on Jewish Material Claims Against Germany, "Position Paper – Slave Labor," 15 June 1999.

[78] "We Condemn Syria's Denial of the Holocaust," in *New York Times* (9 February 2000). To document "increased anti-Semitism" in Europe, David Harris of the AJC pointed to relatively strong survey support for the statement that "Jews are exploiting the memory of the Nazi extermination of the Jews for their own purposes." He also adduced the "extremely negative way that some German papers reported on the Jewish Claims Conference . . . during the recent negotiations over compensation for slave and forced labor. Numerous stories depicted the Claims Conference itself and the mostly Jewish lawyers as greedy and self-serving, and a bizarre discussion ensued in mainstream

The shakedown of Switzerland and Germany has been only a prelude to the grand finale: the shakedown of Eastern Europe. With the collapse of the Soviet bloc, alluring prospects opened up in the former heartland of European Jewry. Cloaking itself in the sanctimonious mantle of "needy Holocaust victims," the Holocaust industry has sought to extort billions of dollars from these already impoverished countries. Pursuing this end with reckless and ruthless abandon, it has become the main fomenter of anti-Semitism in Europe.

The Holocaust industry has positioned itself as the sole legitimate claimant to all the communal and private assets of those who perished during the Nazi holocaust. "It has been agreed with the Government of Israel," Edgar Bronfman told the House Banking Committee, "that heirless assets should accrue to the World Jewish Restitution Organization." Using this "mandate," the Holocaust industry has called on former Soviet-bloc countries to hand over all prewar Jewish properties or come up with monetary compensation.[79] Unlike in the case of

---

newspapers about whether there are as many Jewish survivors as cited by the Claims Conference." (Hearings before the Foreign Relations Committee, United States Senate, 5 April 2000) In fact, I found it nearly impossible to raise this matter in Germany. Although the taboo was finally broken by the liberal German daily *Die Berliner Zeitung*, the courage displayed by its editor, Martin Sueskind, and US correspondent, Stefan Elfenbein, found only a faint echo in the German media, in large part owing to the legal threats and moral blackmail of the Claims Conference as well as the general German reluctance to openly criticize Jews.

[79] Hearings before the Committee on Banking and Financial Services, House of Representatives, 11 December 1996. J.D. Bindenagel (ed.), *Proceedings, Washington Conference on Holocaust-Era Assets: 30 November–3 December 1998* (US Government Printing Office: Washington, DC), 687, 700–1, 706.

Switzerland and Germany, however, it makes these demands away from the glare of publicity. Public opinion has so far not been averse to the blackmailing of Swiss bankers and German industrialists, but it might look less kindly on the blackmailing of starving Polish peasants. Jews who lost family members during the Nazi holocaust might also take a jaundiced view of the WJRO's machinations. Claiming to be the legitimate heir of those who perished in order to appropriate their assets could easily be mistaken for grave-robbery. On the other hand, the Holocaust industry doesn't need a mobilized public opinion. With the support of key US officials, it can easily break the feeble resistance of already prostrate nations.

"It is important to recognize that our efforts at communal property restitution," Stuart Eizenstat told a House committee, "are integral to the rebirth and renewal of Jewish life" in Eastern Europe. Allegedly to "promote the revival" of Jewish life in Poland, the World Jewish Restitution Organization is demanding title over the 6,000 prewar communal Jewish properties, including those currently being used as hospitals and schools. The prewar Jewish population of Poland stood at 3.5 million; the current population is several thousand. Does reviving Jewish life really require one synagogue or school building per Polish Jew? The organization is also laying claim to hundreds of thousands of parcels of Polish land valued in the many tens of billions of dollars. "Polish officials fear," *Jewish Week* reports, that the demand "could bankrupt the nation." When Poland's Parliament proposed limits on compensation to avert insolvency, Elan Steinberg of the WJC denounced the legislation as "fundamentally an anti-American act."[80]

---

[80] Hearings before International Relations Committee, House of Representatives,

Tightening the screws on Poland, Holocaust industry attorneys filed a class-action lawsuit in Judge Korman's court to compensate "aging and dying Holocaust survivors." The complaint charged that the postwar Polish governments "continued during the last fifty-four years" a genocidal "expulsion to extinction" policy against Jews. New York City Council members jumped in with a unanimous resolution calling on Poland "to pass comprehensive legislation providing for the complete restitution of Holocaust assets," while 57 members of Congress (led by Congressman Anthony Weiner of New York) dispatched a letter to the Polish Parliament demanding "comprehensive legislation that would return 100% of all property and assets seized during the Holocaust." "As the people involved are getting older and older every day," the letter said, "time is running out to compensate those wronged."[81]

---

6 August 1998. Bindenagel, *Washington Conference on Holocaust-Era Assets*, 433. Joan Gralia, "Poland Tries to Get Holocaust Lawsuit Dismissed," in *Reuters* (23 December 1999). Eric J. Greenberg, "Polish Restitution Plan Slammed," in *Jewish Week* (14 January 2000). "Poland Limits WWII Compensation Plan," in *Newsday* (6 January 2000).

[81] *Theo Garb et al. v. Republic of Poland* (United States District Court, Eastern District of New York, June 18, 1999). (The class-action lawsuit was brought by Edward E. Klein and Mel Urbach, the latter a veteran of the Swiss and German settlements. An "amended complaint" submitted on 2 March 2000 was joined by many more lawyers but omits some of the more colorful charges against the postwar Polish governments.) "Dear Leads NYC Council in Call to Polish Government to Make Restitution to Victims of Holocaust Era Property Seizure," in *News From Council Member Noach Dear* (29 November 1999). (The textual quote is from the actual resolution, No. 1072, adopted on 23 November 1999.) "[Anthony D.] Weiner Urges Polish Government To Repatriate Holocaust Claims," US House of Representatives (press release, 14

Testifying before the Senate Banking Committee, Stuart Eizenstat deplored the lax pace of evictions in Eastern Europe: "A variety of problems have arisen in the return of properties. For example, in some countries, when persons or communities have attempted to reclaim properties, they have been asked, sometimes required . . . to allow current tenants to remain for a lengthy period of time at rent-controlled rates."[82] The delinquency of Belarus particularly exercised Eizenstat. Belarus is "very, very far" behind in handing over prewar Jewish properties, he told the House International Relations Committee.[83] The average monthly income of a Belarussian is $100.

To force submission from recalcitrant governments, the Holocaust industry wields the bludgeon of US sanctions. Eizenstat urged Congress to "elevate" Holocaust compensation, put it "high on the list" of requirements for those East European countries that are seeking entry into the OECD, the WTO, the European Union, NATO, and the Council of Europe: "They will listen if you speak. . . . They will get the hint." Israel Singer of the WJC called on Congress to "continue looking at the shopping list" in order to "check" that every country pays up. "It is extremely important that the countries involved in the issue understand," Congressman Benjamin Gilman of the House International Relations Committee said, "that their response . . . is one of several standards by which the United States assesses its

---

October 1999). (The textual quotes are from the press release and actual letter, dated 13 October 1999.)

[82] Hearings before the Committee on Banking, Housing, and Urban Affairs, United States Senate, 23 April 1996.

[83] Hearings before the International Relations Committee, House of Representatives, 6 August 1998.

bilateral relationship." Avraham Hirschson, chairman of Israel's Knesset Committee on Restitution and Israel's representative on the World
Jewish Restitution Organization, paid tribute to Congressional complicity in the shakedown. Recalling his "fights" with the Romanian
Prime Minister, Hirschson testified: "But I ask one remark, in the
middle of the fighting, and it changed that atmosphere. I told him,
you know, in two days I am going to be in a hearing here in Congress.
What do you want me to tell them in the hearing? Whole atmosphere
was changed." The World Jewish Congress has "created an entire
Holocaust industry," a lawyer for survivors warns, and is "guilty of
promoting . . . a very ugly resurgence of anti-Semitism in Europe."[84]

"Were it not for the United States of America," Eizenstat aptly
observed in his paean to Congress, "very few, if any, of these activities
would be ongoing today." To justify the pressures exerted on Eastern
Europe, he explained that a hallmark of "Western" morality is to
"return or pay compensation for communal and private property
wrongfully appropriated." For the "new democracies" in Eastern
Europe, meeting this standard "would be commensurate with their
passage from totalitarianism to democratic states." Eizenstat is a senior
US government official and a prominent supporter of Israel. Yet,
judging by the respective claims of Native Americans and Palestinians,
neither the US nor Israel has yet made the transition.[85]

---

[84] Hearings before the International Relations Committee, House of Representatives, 6 August 1998. Isabel Vincent, "Who Will Reap the Nazi-Era
Reparations?" in *National Post* (20 February 1999).
[85] Hearings before the International Relations Committee, House of Representatives, 6 August 1998. Currently an honorary vice-president of the American

In his House testimony, Hirschson conjured the melancholy spectacle of aging "needy Holocaust victims" from Poland "coming to me to my office in the Knesset each day . . . begging to get back what belongs to them . . . to get back the houses they left, to get back the stores they left." Meanwhile, the Holocaust industry wages battle on a second front. Repudiating the specious mandate of the World Jewish Restitution Organization, local Jewish communities in Eastern Europe have staked out their own claims on heirless Jewish assets. To benefit from such a claim, however, a Jew must formally adhere to the local Jewish community. The hoped-for revival of Jewish life is thus coming to pass as Eastern European Jews parlay their newly discovered roots into a cut of the Holocaust booty.[86]

The Holocaust industry boasts of earmarking compensation monies for charitable Jewish causes. "While charity is a noble cause," a lawyer representing the actual victims observes, "it is wrong to perform it with other people's money." One favorite cause is "Holocaust education" – the "greatest legacy of our efforts," according to Eizenstat. Hirschson is also founder of an organization called "March of the Living," a centerpiece of Holocaust education and a major beneficiary of compensation monies. In this Zionist-inspired spectacle with a cast of thousands, Jewish youth from around the world converge on the

---

Jewish Committee, Eizenstat was the first chairman of the AJC's Institute on American Jewish–Israeli Relations.

[86] Hearings before the International Relations Committee, House of Representatives, 6 August 1998. Marilyn Henry, "Whose Claim Is It Anyway?" in *Jerusalem Post* (4 July 1997). Bindenagel, *Washington Conference on Holocaust-Era Assets*, 705. Editorial, "Jewish Property Belongs to Jews," in *Haaretz* (26 October 1999).

death camps in Poland for first-hand instruction in Gentile wickedness before being flown off to Israel for salvation. The *Jerusalem Report* captures this Holocaust kitsch moment on the March: " 'I'm so scared, I can't go on, I want to be in Israel already,' repeats a young Connecticut woman over and over. Her body is shaking. . . . Suddenly her friend pulls out a large Israeli flag. She wraps it around the two of them and they move on." An Israeli flag: don't leave home without it.[87]

Speaking at the Washington Conference on Holocaust-Era Assets, David Harris of the AJC waxed eloquent on the "profound impact" pilgrimages to Nazi death camps have on Jewish youth. The *Forward* took note of an episode particularly fraught with pathos. Under the headline "Israeli Teens Frolic With Strippers After Auschwitz Visit," the newspaper explained that, according to experts, the kibbutz students "hired strippers to release the troubling emotions raised by the trip." These same torments apparently racked Jewish students on a US Holocaust Memorial Museum field trip who, according to the *Forward*, "were running around and having a wonderful time and feeling each other up and whatever."[88] Who can doubt the wisdom of

---

[87] Sergio Karas, "Unsettled Accounts," in *Globe and Mail* (1 September 1998). Stuart Eizenstat, "Remarks," Conference on Jewish Material Claims Against Germany and Austria Annual Meeting (New York: 14 July 1999). Tom Sawicki, "6,000 Witnesses," in *Jerusalem Report* (5 May 1994).

[88] Bindenagel, *Washington Conference on Holocaust-Era Assets*, 146. Michael Arnold, "Israeli Teens Frolic With Strippers After Auschwitz Visit," in *Forward* (26 November 1999). Manhattan Congresswoman Carolyn Maloney proudly informed the House Banking Committee of a bill she introduced, the Holocaust Education Act, which "will provide grants through the Department of Education to Holocaust organizations for teacher training, and provide

the Holocaust industry's decision to earmark compensation monies for Holocaust education rather than "fritter away the funds" (Nahum Goldmann) on survivors of Nazi death camps?[89]

In January 2000 officials from nearly fifty states, including Prime Minister Ehud Barak of Israel, attended a major Holocaust education conference in Stockholm. The conference's final declaration underlined the international community's "solemn responsibility" to fight the evils of genocide, ethnic cleansing, racism and xenophobia. A Swedish reporter afterward asked Barak about the Palestinian refugees. On principle, Barak replied, he was against even one refugee coming to Israel: "We cannot accept moral, legal, or other responsibility for refugees." Plainly the conference was a huge success.[90]

The Jewish Claims Conference's official *Guide to Compensation and Restitution for Holocaust Survivors* lists scores of organizational affiliates. A vast, well-heeled bureaucracy has sprung up. Insurance companies, banks, art museums, private industry, tenants and farmers in nearly

---

materials to schools and communities that increase Holocaust education." Representing a city with a public school system notoriously lacking basic teachers and textbooks, Maloney might have set different priorities for scarce Department of Education funds. (Hearings before the Committee on Banking and Financial Services, House of Representatives, 9 February 2000)

[89] Zweig, *German Reparations and the Jewish World*, 118. Goldmann was founder of the World Jewish Congress and the first president of the Claims Conference.

[90] Marilyn Henry, "International Holocaust Education Conference Begins," in *Jerusalem Post* (26 January 2000). Marilyn Henry, "PM: We Have No Moral Obligation to Refugees," in *Jerusalem Post* (27 January 2000). Marilyn Henry, "Holocaust 'Must Be Seared in Collective Memory,'" in *Jerusalem Post* (30 January 2000).

every European country are under the Holocaust industry gun. But the "needy Holocaust victims" in whose name the Holocaust industry acts complain that it is "just perpetuating the expropriation." Many have filed suit against the Claims Conference. The Holocaust may yet turn out to be the "greatest robbery in the history of mankind."[91]

When Israel first entered into negotiations with Germany for reparations after the war, historian Ilan Pappe reports, Foreign Minister Moshe Sharett proposed transferring a part to Palestinian refugees, "in order to rectify what has been called the small injustice (the Palestinian tragedy), caused by the more terrible one (the Holocaust)."[92] Nothing ever came of the proposal. A prominent Israeli academic has suggested using some of the funds from the Swiss banks and German firms for the "compensation of Palestinian Arab refugees."[93] Given that almost all survivors of the Nazi holocaust have already passed away, this would seem to be a sensible proposal.

---

[91] Claims Conference, *Guide to Compensation and Restitution of Holocaust Survivors* (New York: n.d.). Vincent, *Hitler's Silent Partners*, 302 ("expropriation"); cf. 308–9. Ralf Eibl, "Die Jewish Claims Conference ringt um ihren Leumund. Nachkommen jüdischer Sklaven. . . .," in *Die Welt* (8 March 2000) (lawsuits). The Holocaust compensation industry is a taboo subject in the United States. The H-Holocaust web site (*www2.h-net.msu.edu*), for example, barred critical postings even if fully supported with documentary evidence (personal correspondence with board member Richard S. Levy, 19–21 November 1999).

[92] Ilan Pappe, *The Making of the Arab–Israeli Conflict, 1947–51* (London: 1992), 268.

[93] Clinton Bailey, "Holocaust Funds to Palestinians May Meet Some Cost of Compensation," in *International Herald Tribune*; reprinted in *Jordan Times* (20 June 1999).

In vintage WJC style, Israel Singer made the "startling announce-ment" on 13 March 2000 that a newly declassified US document revealed that Austria was holding heirless Holocaust-era assets of Jews worth yet another $10 billion. Singer also charged that "fifty percent of America's total art is looted Jewish art."[94] The Holocaust industry has clearly gone berserk.

[94] Elli Wohlgelernter, "WJC: Austria Holding $10b. In Holocaust Victims' Assets," in *Jerusalem Post* (14 March 2000). In his subsequent Congressional testimony, Singer highlighted the allegation against Austria but – typically – maintained a discreet silence on the charges against the US. (Hearings before the Foreign Relations Committee, United States Senate, 6 April 2000)

CONCLUSION

I t remains to consider the impact of The Holocaust in the United States. In doing so, I also want to engage Peter Novick's own critical remarks on the topic.

Apart from Holocaust memorials, fully seventeen states mandate or recommend Holocaust programs in their schools, and many colleges and universities have endowed chairs in Holocaust studies. Hardly a week passes without a major Holocaust-related story in the *New York Times*. The number of scholarly studies devoted to the Nazi Final Solution is conservatively estimated at over 10,000. Consider by comparison scholarship on the hecatomb in the Congo. Between 1891 and 1911, some 10 million Africans perished in the course of Europe's exploitation of Congolese ivory and rubber resources. Yet, the first and only scholarly volume in English directly devoted to this topic was published two years ago.[1]

Given the vast number of institutions and professionals dedicated

---

[1] Adam Hochschild, *King Leopold's Ghost* (Boston: 1998).

to preserving its memory, The Holocaust is by now firmly entrenched in American life. Novick expresses misgivings, however, whether this is a good thing. In the first place, he cites numerous instances of its sheer vulgarization. Indeed, one is hard-pressed to name a single political cause, whether it be pro-life or pro-choice, animal rights or states' rights, that hasn't conscripted The Holocaust. Decrying the tawdry purposes to which The Holocaust is put, Elie Wiesel declared, "I swear to avoid . . . vulgar spectacles."[2] Yet Novick reports that "the most imaginative and subtle Holocaust photo op came in 1996 when Hillary Clinton, then under heavy fire for various alleged misdeeds, appeared in the gallery of the House during her husband's (much televised) State of the Union Address, flanked by their daughter, Chelsea, and Elie Wiesel."[3] For Hillary Clinton, Kosovo refugees put to flight by Serbia during the NATO bombing recalled Holocaust scenes in *Schindler's List*. "People who learn history from Spielberg movies," a Serbian dissident tartly rejoined, "should not tell us how to live our lives."[4]

The "pretense that the Holocaust is an American memory," Novick further argues, is a moral evasion. It "leads to the shirking of those responsibilities that *do* belong to Americans as they confront their past, their present, and their future." (emphasis in original)[5] He makes an important point. It is much easier to deplore the crimes of others than to look at ourselves. It is also true, however, that were the will

---

[2] Wiesel, *Against Silence*, v. iii, 190; cf. v. i, 186, v. ii, 82, v. iii, 242, and Wiesel, *And the Sea*, 18.

[3] Novick, *The Holocaust*, 230–1.

[4] *New York Times* (25 May 1999).

[5] Novick, *The Holocaust*, 15.

there we could learn much about ourselves from the Nazi experience. Manifest Destiny anticipated nearly all the ideological and programmatic elements of Hitler's *Lebensraum* policy. In fact, Hitler modeled his conquest of the East on the American conquest of the West.[6] During the first half of this century, a majority of American states enacted sterilization laws and tens of thousands of Americans were involuntarily sterilized. The Nazis explicitly invoked this US precedent when they enacted their own sterilization laws.[7] The notorious 1935 Nuremberg Laws stripped Jews of the franchise and forbade miscegenation between Jews and non-Jews. Blacks in the American South suffered the same legal disabilities and were the object of much greater spontaneous and sanctioned popular violence than the Jews in prewar Germany.[8]

To highlight unfolding crimes abroad, the US often summons memories of The Holocaust. The more revealing point, however, is

[6] John Toland, *Adolf Hitler* (New York: 1976), 702. Joachim Fest, *Hitler* (New York: 1975), 214, 650. See also Finkelstein, *Image and Reality*, chap. 4.

[7] See, for example, Stefan Kühl, *The Nazi Connection* (Oxford: 1994).

[8] See, for example, Leon F. Litwack, *Trouble in Mind* (New York: 1998), esp. chaps 5–6. The vaunted Western tradition is deeply implicated in Nazism as well. To justify the extermination of the handicapped – the precursor of the Final Solution – Nazi doctors deployed the concept "life unworthy of life" (*lebensunwertes Leben*). In *Gorgias*, Plato wrote: "I can't see that life is worth living if a person's body is in a terrible state." In *The Republic*, Plato sanctioned the murder of defective children. On a related point, Hitler's opposition in *Mein Kampf* to birth control on the ground that it preempts natural selection was prefigured by Rousseau in his *Discourse on the Origins of Inequality*. Shortly after World War II, Hannah Arendt reflected that "the subterranean stream of Western history has finally come to the surface and usurped the dignity of our tradition" (*Origins of Totalitarianism*, ix).

when the US invokes The Holocaust. Crimes of official enemies such
as the Khmer Rouge bloodbath in Cambodia, the Soviet invasion of
Afghanistan, the Iraqi invasion of Kuwait, and Serbian ethnic cleansing
in Kosovo recall The Holocaust; crimes in which the US is complicit
do not.

Just as the Khmer Rouge atrocities were unfolding in Cambodia,
the US-backed Indonesian government was slaughtering one-third
of the population in East Timor. Yet unlike Cambodia, the East
Timor genocide did not rate comparison with The Holocaust; it
didn't even rate news coverage.[9] Just as the Soviet Union was
committing what the Simon Wiesenthal Center called "another
genocide" in Afghanistan, the US-backed regime in Guatemala was
perpetrating what the Guatemalan Truth Commission recently called
a "genocide" against the indigenous Mayan population. President
Reagan dismissed the charges against the Guatemalan government
as a "bum rap." To honor Jeane Kirkpatrick's achievement as
chief Reagan Administration apologist for the unfolding crimes in
Central America, the Simon Wiesenthal Center awarded her the
Humanitarian of the Year Award.[10] Simon Wiesenthal was privately
beseeched before the award ceremony to reconsider. He refused.
Elie Wiesel was privately asked to intercede with the Israeli government, a main weapons supplier for the Guatemalan butchers. He
too refused. The Carter Administration invoked the memory of The

[9] See, for example, Edward Herman and Noam Chomsky, *The Political Economy
of Human Rights*, v. i: *The Washington Connection and Third World Fascism*
(Boston: 1979), 129–204.
[10] *Response* (March 1983 and January 1986).

Holocaust as it sought haven for Vietnamese "boat people" fleeing the Communist regime. The Clinton Administration forgot The Holocaust as it forced back Haitian "boat people" fleeing US-supported death squads.[11]

Holocaust memory loomed large as the US-led NATO bombing of Serbia commenced in the spring of 1999. As we have seen, Daniel Goldhagen compared Serbian crimes against Kosovo with the Final Solution and, at President Clinton's bidding, Elie Wiesel journeyed to Kosovar refugee camps in Macedonia and Albania. Already before Wiesel went to shed tears on cue for the Kosovars, however, the US-backed Indonesian regime had resumed where it left off in the late 1970s, perpetrating new massacres in East Timor. The Holocaust vanished from memory, however, as the Clinton Administration acquiesced in the bloodletting. "Indonesia matters," a Western diplomat explained, "and East Timor doesn't."[12]

Novick points to passive US complicity in human disasters dissimilar in other respects yet comparable in scale to the Nazi extermination. Recalling, for example, the million children killed in the Final Solution, he observes that American presidents do little more than utter pieties as, worldwide, many times that number of children "die of malnutrition and preventable diseases" every year.[13] One might also consider a pertinent case of *active* US complicity. After the United States-led coalition devastated Iraq in 1991 to punish

[11] Noam Chomsky, *Turning the Tide* (Boston: 1985), 36 (Wiesel cited from interview in the Hebrew press). Berenbaum, *World Must Know*, 3.

[12] *Financial Times* (8 September 1999).

[13] Novick, *The Holocaust*, 255.

"Saddam-Hitler," the United States and Britain forced murderous UN sanctions on that hapless country in an attempt to depose him. As in the Nazi holocaust, a million children have likely perished.[14] Questioned on national television about the grisly death toll in Iraq, Secretary of State Madeleine Albright replied that "the price is worth it."

"The very extremity of the Holocaust," Novick argues, "seriously limit[s] its capacity to provide lessons applicable to our everyday world." As the "benchmark of oppression and atrocity," it tends to "trivializ[e] crimes of lesser magnitude."[15] Yet the Nazi holocaust can also sensitize us to these injustices. Seen through the lens of Auschwitz, what previously was taken for granted – for example, bigotry – no longer can be.[16] In fact, it was the Nazi holocaust that discredited the scientific racism that was so pervasive a feature of American intellectual life before World War II.[17]

For those committed to human betterment, a touchstone of evil does not preclude but rather invites comparisons. Slavery occupied roughly the same place in the moral universe of the late nineteenth century as the Nazi holocaust does today. Accordingly, it was often invoked to illuminate evils not fully appreciated. John Stuart Mill compared the condition of women in that most hallowed Victorian institution, the family, to slavery. He even ventured that in crucial respects it was worse. "I am far from pretending that wives are in

[14] See, for example, Geoff Simons, *The Scourging of Iraq* (New York: 1998).
[15] Novick, *The Holocaust*, 244, 14.
[16] On this point, see esp. Chaumont, *La concurrence*, 316–18.
[17] See, for example, Carl N. Degler, *In Search of Human Nature* (Oxford: 1991), 202ff.

DEMCO